COLUMBIA
ECUADOR
Iquitos
LORETO
PERU
BRAZIL
Chiclayo
Lima
Pacific Ocean
Ica
Cuzco
BOLIVIA

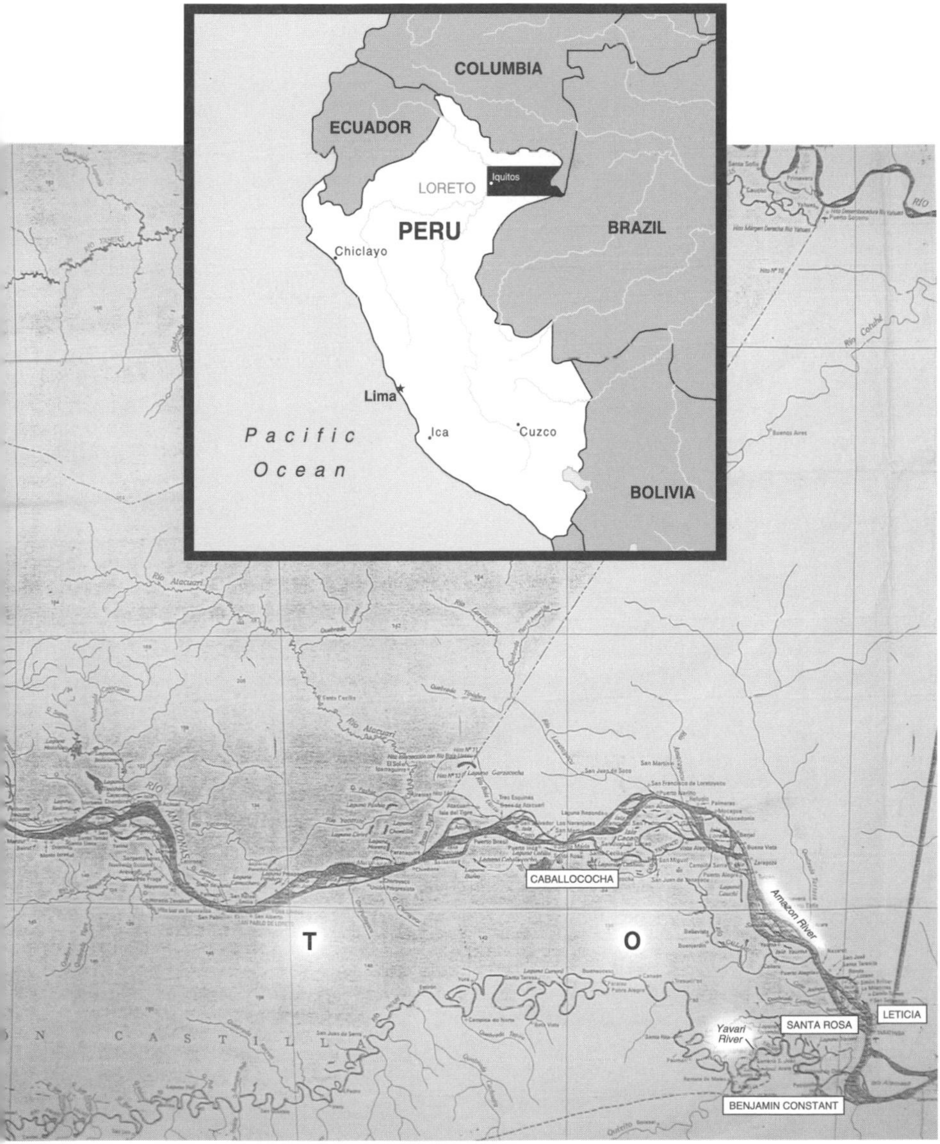

RÍO AMAZONAS
CABALLOCOCHA
Amazon River
T
O
LETICIA
SANTA ROSA
Yavari River
BENJAMIN CONSTANT
N C A S T I L L A

IF GOD SHOULD CHOOSE

THE AUTHORIZED STORY OF JIM AND RONI BOWERS

KRISTEN STAGG

MOODY PRESS
CHICAGO

ISBN: 0-8024-1588-1

1 3 5 7 9 10 8 6 4 2

Printed in the United States of America

Dedicated to
Veronica Lynn Bowers and Charity Lynn Bowers,
who live on in the memories of those they left behind,
And to the Peruvians living along the Amazon River,
those who already know Jesus Christ as personal Savior,
and many more who still need to hear the good news of salvation.

FOREWORD

Moments before the funeral service for Roni Bowers was to begin, I was escorted through the corridors of Marcus Pointe Baptist Church in Pensacola, Florida to meet Jim and the family members that accompanied him on that very difficult day. Like the rest of the nation, I had heard of the tragedy and caught bits and pieces of the troubling story on national newscasts. When I learned that Jim had expressed a desire to have me be part of the service, I felt a special urgency to attend. Not only was Jim a brother in Christ, he was a fellow MK. Children of missionary parents (or MK's) share a unique bond. We are third culture kids who were raised overseas and many of us spent our childhood in boarding schools far away from home. Whenever we meet there is an instant connection and a look of gratitude to find someone that shares and understands so much of our own story.

As I walked into the room, Jim stepped forward to shake my hand. We embraced. After a few moments of conversation I asked him if there was anything in particular he would like me to sing. He said that he had attended several concerts and would prefer that I choose what I believed would be most appropriate. As the service began I still had not settled on the right selections. I have been privileged to record songs of comfort for those suffering the ache of loss and songs of encouragement for the grief-stricken, songs of hope and reminders of God's promise to convey us safely to heaven's shores. I ran through the titles and lyrics in my mind.

Jim made his way to the platform and every eye was fixed on him. There had been several speakers, but everyone was waiting to hear from the one who had been in that plane and experienced the terrifying horror of being shot down, the one who had pulled his wife and child's bodies from the wreckage. What would he say? We watched closely for a facial expression that would give us an idea of what he was feeling. Without drama, sensationalism or any attempt to garner sympathy, Jim spoke simply of the providence of God evident throughout the whole ordeal. He read a list of all the details and ways God had been at work.

The word providence appears only once in the New Testament, in Acts 24:2. Providence means forethought or provision to consider in advance or to look out for beforehand. The Westminster Shorter Catechism affirms that "God's works of providence are the acts of his most holy, wise, and powerful preserving and governing all his creatures, and all their actions." Hence, as Thomas Watson reminds us, there is no such thing as blind fate; rather a sovereign God guides and governs the world, ordering all things after the counsel of His own will, to His own glory. Who is to blame for the seeming chaotic chain of events that led to Roni and Charity's deaths? While God's providence permits men's sins and wrongdoing, He has no hand in their sins. While He may have a hand in the action where sin is, He has no hand in the sin of the action (Thomas Watson).

A Peruvian official sat in the front pew and I wondered what impact Jim's words were having on him. Jim's powerful and clear testimony that day cast no blame on the Peruvian air force pilots, nor was there ever a hint of bitterness against God. While humbly acknowledging that the mystery of God's providence is veiled from our present understanding, he recognized that faith is continuing to acquiesce in His will and trust in His goodness. It is impossible to judge all of God's working by the fragments and pieces of our own experiences, but when we finally reach heaven, I'm sure we will marvel at the glory of God's sovereign working and see wonder and mercy in all of His providence.

As Jim finished speaking, I settled on the song "Find Us Faithful." With imagery from Hebrews 11, the song is a cry to God for strength and help to finish well this sacred journey of faith, and a statement of complete trust regardless of what God providentially allows along the way.

ACKNOWLEDGMENTS

This book never could have been written without a great deal of help from many people. In addition to the gracious hand of God giving me ability beyond myself, I owe an enormous debt of gratitude to the following people for their contributions:

Jim Bell and Greg Thornton at Moody Press for their helpful suggestions and encouragement;

Jim and Roni's families, who not only shared memories and mementos with me at a time when their pain was still fresh and raw, but also graciously extended hospitality to me: Wilma Bowers, Phil Bowers, and Dan Bowers; John and Gloria Luttig, Garnett Luttig Jr., and Pat Luttig;

Bob Buyers, Carol Stagg, and Debbie Warner for typing reams of material and finding important addresses while I was working in seclusion;

Friends and colleagues of the Bowers family, for contributing recollections as well as e-mails, videotapes, photos, maps, and letters:

In the United States: Rev. Dave Buckley, Sherie Carico, Jim Cross, Dan and Heidi and Ryan Enck, Rev. Gordon Godfrey, Pam Hewitt, Jennifer Kalnbach, Jim and Paula Kramer, Andy and Di Large, Chuck and Carrie Porter, Bill & Pat Rexford, Todd and Mary Beth Rexford, Dr. Bill Rudd, Steve and Betty and Scott Schaub, Dave Southwell, and Debbie Walsh;

In Peru: Connie Adams, Omar Curmayari Aricari, Pastor Edwin Chavez, Kevin and Bobbi Donaldson, Rich and Dee Donaldson, Arodi Fasanando, Hugo ans Micaela Fasanando, Melvina Fasanando, Pastor Ernesto Flores, Neil and Sandy Heim, Darlene Hull, Larry and Carolyn Hultquist, Pastor Javier and Karina Manihuari, Kay Panaggio, Pastor Juan Pedro, Lynn Porter, Pastor Carlos Rubio, Teodora Sifuentes, and Marcos Vela;

K. Michael Cole, for photocopying stacks of newspaper articles early in the fact-gathering stage;

My cousin, Jeff Dernlan, and Randall Dennis, for helping me trace music copyright ownership to Gaither Music Management, where Jeremy Stockwell granted usage permission;

Lynn Porter for translating in Peru, enabling me to converse with Peruvians whose contributions are such a vital part of this book;

Susan and Tony, for loaning the serene and beautiful setting in which to create;

Stagg family members, for understanding the time pressures and allowing me to say no to scheduled events (even when some of you were leaving the country for a year), and for praying as you saw my hair—literally—stand on end: Mom and Dad, Kathy, Karen and Don, Paul, and Mandi;

Jeannie Lockerbie Stephenson, for bearing the burden of my workload during the months I was interviewing and writing;

My prayer partners, for your faithful support and letters and phone calls of encouragement during some very difficult days: Cathy, Christine, David, Debbie, Don, Donna, Faith, Jackie, Jennifer, Kent, Penny, Susan, Toby, and Traci. Many others added me to their prayer lists, and I needed every single prayer you said for me;

Most of all, thank you, Jim and Cory, for reliving difficult memories; for trusting me with this story; for allowing me access to all the people who would help me tell it accurately and completely; and for making it possible to meet your friends and see your work along the river firsthand. Because of this, my life has been changed forever.

I WILL SERVE THE LORD

There marches through the centuries the martyrs of the cross,
All those who chose to follow Christ, to suffer any loss.
And though their journey led them through the shadowlands of death,
The song of their commitment they rehearsed with every breath.

Chorus
I will serve the Lord. I will serve the Lord, my God.
And if God should choose and my life I lose,
Though my foe may slay me, I will serve the Lord.

Uncertain days now echo back that strong and urgent strain,
To count the cost, take up the cross and join in the refrain.
For should our journey lead us through the shadowlands of death,
May this be our hearts' resolve as long as we have breath:

Chorus
I will serve the Lord. I will serve the Lord, my God.
And if God should choose and my life I lose,
Though my foe may slay me, I will serve the Lord.

The honor and the privilege ours; with wounds we suffer by His side.
And to the glory of the Lord, those sacred scars we wear with pride.

Chorus
I will serve the Lord. I will serve the Lord, my God.
And if God should choose and my life I lose,
Though my foe may slay me, I will serve the Lord.

Chapter One

There marches through the centuries
the martyrs of the cross . . .

"They're killing us! They're killing us!" The voice yelling in Spanish over the radio sounded Peruvian, but it belonged to an American missionary pilot. He was trying to contact the control tower in Iquitos, Peru, to alert someone—anyone—to the grave danger he and his passengers faced.

Missionaries Jim and Veronica "Roni" Bowers, their young son, Cory, and infant daughter, Charity, were flying back to Iquitos with pilot and coworker Kevin Donaldson. All of them belonged to the Association of Baptists for World Evangelism, Inc. (ABWE), an independent Baptist mission organization based in Harrisburg, Pennsylvania. The group had flown the day before to the border Peru shares with Brazil to conduct business, and were less than an hour from home and lunch when tragedy struck the single-engine Cessna floatplane in which they traveled.

It struck in a hailstorm of bullets from a Peruvian air force jet. The A-37 fighter appeared briefly behind and off to one side of the Cessna and then the other. Before the missionaries could find out from Iquitos what the air force was doing or what it might want with them, bullets slammed into the missionary plane.

As Kevin plummeted toward the rain forest, he prayed that he could glide to water and land the floatplane. He shut off the engine and fuel lines to prevent the awful possibility of fire. At least one of the A-37's machine-gun bullets already had pierced a fuel line, and Kevin's safety measures were too late to prevent the billowing smoke and flames that eventually engulfed the cabin.

Why are the pilots shooting at us? Jim Bowers wondered. *Why would they shoot us down over trees when this plane is equipped with floats? Are they trying to kill us? Why would they be concerned about missionaries anyway?*

Because the Bowers family was committed to following God, whatever He asked them to do, it was hard to make sense of the nightmarish events taking place in the sky over the Amazon jungle.

James Alan Bowers was born two weeks into the new year of 1963. At ten months of age, he left the United States with his parents and two-year-old brother, Phil, for Brazil, where Terry and Wilma had been assigned as missionaries with the Association of Baptists for World Evangelism (ABWE).

Terry was appointed to the work in Brazil where Hank Scheltema, a college friend, had inaugurated the mission's aviation ministry two years earlier. ABWE's president, Dr. Harold T. Commons, had asked another young pilot to open the Baptist mission's aviation work in South America, but Nate Saint was already headed to a South American country with a different mission board and politely declined. Nate was killed in 1956 with four other colleagues while attempting to reach the fierce Waorani tribe (commonly called Aucas by outsiders) with the message of salvation through Jesus Christ. God used Nate's martyrdom in Ecuador to influence Terry Bowers to become a missionary pilot.

Terry met Wilma Herman at Calvary Baptist Church in

Muskegon, Michigan. Wilma had practically grown up in the church. Her father was a deacon, and the Hermans often invited missionaries to eat with them and stay in their home. She attended a camp every year in Lake Ann, Michigan, where missionary speakers were a regular feature. During the summer before her senior year of high school, Wilma sat under a tree and prayed, "Dear God, if You want me to be a missionary, I will go." She didn't know if that was what God wanted her to do, but she wanted Him to know that she would do whatever He asked of her, including foreign missionary service.

When Terry and Wilma met, he had just been discharged from active duty in the U.S. Navy. He had observed missionaries at work while serving in the Far East, and it seemed to Terry that God might want him to be a missionary someday. Terry trained in missionary aviation at Moody Bible Institute, the school where he and Wilma met Hank and Ruth Scheltema.

Terry and Wilma married in 1959 and began looking around at evangelical mission boards. They settled on ABWE, the same organization Hank and Ruth Scheltema had joined. ABWE not only permitted its pilots to be involved in evangelism and church planting; it was one of the founding principles of the mission that all missionaries, no matter what their training or background, actively disciple individuals and help start churches.

The Association of Baptists for Evangelism in the Orient (as ABWE was first known) had its genesis in 1927 when missionaries working at a hospital in the Philippines refused to follow their denomination's instructions to quit preaching and focus only on the Filipinos' social needs. Recognizing that the social ills of any society would never change apart from lives being placed under God's control, the missionaries decided to leave their denomination.

Dr. and Mrs. Rafael and Norma Thomas, two of those missionaries, were related to an influential member of the mission society, who also happened to be Norma Thomas's mother. Mrs. Peabody, a retired missionary from India and a driving force in the denomination's mission efforts, also withdrew from the organization. With her close friend, Mrs. Marguerite Doane, Lucy Peabody formed the Association of Baptists for Evangelism in the Orient. As president and financier of the fledgling organization, the two widows with their extensive business experience and personal fortunes supported ABEO's handful of missionaries in the Philippines.

Within twelve years, ABEO had added missionaries in non-Asian countries (the first being Peru in 1939), changed its name to the Association of Baptists for World Evangelism, and had a new president in Harold T. Commons.

Most of the people lived in
rough-hewn wood structures set up on stilts

By the time Terry and Wilma joined ABWE in 1962, the mission agency had more than 200 missionaries in over a dozen countries. The Bowers family was headed to Brazil, where mission stations had been established in São Paulo, the capital, and in the far northern and southern parts of the country. Aviation was still brand-new. Terry would operate a second floatplane for ABWE in the Amazon region of Brazil.

Amazonas, Brazil, was known as one of the world's last frontiers, and rightly so. The hundreds of thousands of acres of towering rain forest were bisected by the winding Amazon River and its many tributaries. The jungle sheltered settlements where Brazilians farmed small plantations of manioc, plantains, and rice to supplement their hunting and fishing.

The jungle canopy also sheltered a diversity of wildlife from capybara (the world's largest rodent) and poisonous snakes to wild pigs, exotic birds, monkeys, and lizards. The region's unfriendly climate—with temperatures hovering near 100 degrees year-round and humidity near 100 percent—bred malaria-bearing mosquitoes, tuberculosis, and cholera, among other diseases.

Most of the people lived in rough-hewn wood structures set up on stilts, with thatched roofs to keep off the rain. Some were enclosed and could rightly be called houses; the rest looked more like shelters since they were open on all sides or had only half walls. The wooden slat floors eliminated the need for indoor plumbing. Sewage collected beneath the homes until annual floods washed it all away. Settlements weren't hacked out of the jungle at the water's edge for nothing; the river served as communal bathhouse, Laundromat, and highway to the towns up and down the river.

For those willing to brave the outwardly harsh conditions, however, the typical friendliness of the Brazilian people more than compensated for any difficulties. The poorest of river dwellers willingly shared what they had with unexpected visitors, even offering lodging to stranded travelers.

The Bowers family discovered that the poverty of the people to whom they came to minister wasn't simply material; it was also spiritual. Superstitions abounded. Fear of evil spirits believed to inhabit the jungle was endemic, and the influence of early Jesuit priests merely overlaid existing animism with Catholic ritual. Overcoming these barriers to accepting the truth of Scripture was every bit as hard as figuring out where the missionaries' limited funds could do the most good.

Terry and Wilma settled into their new home in the town of Benjamin Constant on the banks of the Amazon River. Although they had shipped household goods and foodstuffs from the United States, they often had to fashion what they needed from materials at hand. Terry and several local helpers built a hangar that floated on *massaranduba* trees, used by Brazilians to craft their canoes. The huge logs made an ideal buoyant base for the structure that would house a single-engine floatplane.

While Terry flew up and down the Amazon, ferrying people and supplies to remote spots, Wilma kept house, no small feat in the jungle. Cooking was all done from scratch; there were no mixes or prepared items to speed up the task. Any foods that couldn't be peeled or thoroughly cooked first had to be soaked in an iodine solution to clean off the germs spread by ubiquitous bugs or human feces used to fertilize produce. All drinking water and dishwater had to be boiled to prevent transmission of disease.

Shopping, too, was a complicated business. Open-air markets where flies swarmed over the raw meat (calling it "fresh" might have been a stretch) and produce served as Wilma's local supermarket. Sometimes she could find enough sugar and flour, sometimes not. At least the river provided an unending supply of fresh fish, including the delectable 300-pound specialty: *pirarucú*. Terry told local fishermen, "If you ever catch a *pirarucú* near us, we'll buy a quarter or a half of it." Wilma nearly always had some of that.

It was a laborious job, but Wilma viewed her main task as facilitating Terry's work and making her home a haven for her family. She learned from the other missionaries and from the local women how to make do, or she did without; it was that simple. When she wasn't looking after the house or teaching her children, Wilma helped Brazilian women teach Bible lessons, and she dispensed basic first-aid medicine in the absence of a local doctor.

The Bowers parents expected their boys to obey immediately, respect adults, and generally behave with good manners whether they were among missionaries or Brazilians. They attended the local Baptist church which had been started some years before. The service, although different in format from services back in the United States and conducted in Portuguese, still involved worshiping God. The boys were expected to show proper reverence whether it was their dad preaching or a Brazilian pastor.

As children, Jim and Phil didn't have any heavier responsibilities than most kids. They were home-schooled up to third grade by Wilma, thanks to the Calvert Correspondence School in Baltimore, Maryland. And in their spare time, the boys were free to enjoy their jungle and river playgrounds. They played soccer, swam with their Brazilian friends, or went fishing.

Terry often tied a canoe to one of the plane's floats, flew off to a secluded lake, and treated the boys to fishing in uncharted waters. In some places, the fish literally jumped into the airplane as they landed. Every so often they'd spend the night in the airplane and fly home the following day. Jim grew up in this child's paradise.

But like every human paradise, this one, too, had its serpent. After third grade, the boys went away to boarding school. It was all Wilma could do to take care of the house and Dan, born four years after Jim. She couldn't teach, too.

Jim was only eight when he started at the school for missionary kids (MKs) upriver in Iquitos, Peru. It helped to have Phil there and the Schlener kids, whose parents also were ABWE missionaries in Brazil and lived fairly close to the Bowers family. Tim, Cindi, Leanne, and Rena could commiserate with Jim and Phil, and speak Portuguese among themselves at the school in Spanish-speaking Peru. It wasn't unusual for newcomers to cry themselves to sleep at night, and teenaged Rena took special care of little Jim.

The separation was miserable for parents and children alike. ABWE doesn't require its missionaries to send their children away; each family is allowed to make that decision on their own. In the Amazon region there weren't many schools, and like the people among whom they resided, the foreigners found that daily existence took almost all their time and effort. With toddlers in tow, teaching became impossible for the missionary mothers.

So the Bowers children went across the border to school. They flew home for holidays and summer vacations, where they returned to bedrooms that were exactly as they had left them. Wilma wanted the boys to realize that even though they weren't living at home, they were still part of the family. During their breaks, Phil and Jim accompanied their dad on his speedboat or airplane jaunts to hold church services in the villages where groups of Christians were being formed into new churches. They also joined in the youth activities at the local church and played with their Brazilian friends.

When the boys were at home and their dad had to go somewhere in the plane, they could go along and fish in secluded lakes. On the shorter trips to villages near Benjamin Constant where churches were being started, Terry let the boys fuel up the speedboat and drive to their destination. It was one such occasion that alerted Terry to the fact that Jim's eyesight wasn't quite right.

"Just keep us headed toward that white tree," Terry said, pointing out the distinctive landmark in the distance.

When the speedboat did not maintain course, Terry wanted to know what the problem was. Jim finally admitted, "I don't see what white tree you're talking about!"

On the family's next trip to Lima, Peru, Jim's eye exam revealed—surprise!—that the eight-year-old boy needed glasses.

Jim attended the MK school in Iquitos for one year. After a one-year furlough in Muskegon, Michigan, the Bowers family returned to Brazil in 1973. They were starting their third term of missionary service. Phil and Jim went back to boarding school, but this time to a school in Brazil. New Tribes Mission ran a boarding school for MKs in Puraquequara, named for the electric eels found in the waters around the property. Jim really enjoyed many aspects of this school. There were more than 100 other MKs, giving ample opportunity for activities that weren't available in their homeschool setting, such as organized sports and friendships with other American kids.

Discipline matters at Puraquequara were helped by a system known as gratis. Because the grounds required extensive upkeep, all the children were required to do manual labor. But gratis meant doing heavy work in one-hour segments: mixing cement, clearing jungle growth with machetes, and moving dirt, among many other unpleasant tasks completed under the scorching tropical sun. Gratis duties were served during the time slotted for extracurricular activities, which provided extra incentive to curb problematic behavior.

Jim didn't have to serve much gratis beyond the mandatory two hours on Saturday morning since he wasn't a troublemaker, according to those who knew him then; they found him easy-going and peaceable. Terry and Wilma, too, had to be careful that they didn't automatically assume fighting among their boys wasn't Jim's fault. But most of the time, Jim was more of a nurturer.

Some of the health threats
Jim and his brothers faced
weren't from critters but diseases.

Dan always admired his older brothers. Where Phil's competitive nature forced him to excel in sports, Jim took on more of a protective role and spent time playing with Dan on his level. He didn't mind letting Dan beat him at games in order to make his younger brother feel good about himself. Dan remembers Jim coming to sit on his bed at night during the first months when Dan cried himself to sleep. Once the boys were older, Dan tried to play the guitar and be a role model for the younger kids like Jim.

The Puraquequara school followed a fairly strict routine: up at 7:00 A.M. with fifteen minutes for the MKs to read their Bibles before breakfast. School went from 8:00 A.M. until 3:30 P.M. with a break for lunch. Supper was at 6:00 P.M., followed by two hours of study hall and dorm Bible reading. Lights went out at 9:30 P.M. when the generator was turned off.

Jim spent some of the afternoon hours doing chores or

homework, but that still left time for soccer and basketball, or investigating the natural treasures of the jungle and river. One unique facet of life at Puraquequara is that boys in high school were allowed to bring their shotguns to boarding school, and MKs whose parents worked with Indian tribes brought bows and arrows or dart guns. Jim often went on hunting expeditions where the boys stalked birds, monkeys, rodents, and wild pigs, or anything else that moved through the trees.

Swimming at The Rocks was another favorite pasttime. The Bowers brothers and their friends dove off the pile of rocks into the Amazon River and explored the underwater passageways without a second's thought, although their school had been named for the electric eels that inhabited the area. Students over the age of thirteen were allowed to frequent this spot at night. The Bowers's parents prayed extrahard for the boys' safety, knowing that natural curiosity and fearlessness could lead their children into danger. On one expedition to The Rocks, Jim dove into the water but didn't reappear. The other kids began to panic, but Jim finally surfaced, gasping for air. He'd gotten trapped in one of the underwater caves and couldn't find his way out.

The boys learned early about common sense and safety in their jungle surroundings. Everyone knew that dusk was the time of day to be especially alert for snakes on the prowl for dinner after a day spent warming themselves in the sun. They kept a lookout for scorpions and thorny plants that could cause serious infection.

Some of the health threats Jim and his brothers faced weren't from critters but diseases. During his first year at Puraquequara, one of Jim's three roommates contracted meningitis and died within a matter of days. The students and staff immediately were given oral medication, and the surviving roommates moved to temporary quarters while their room was thoroughly disinfected. The incident served as one of several sobering reminders of the uncertainty and brevity of life.

Terry timed his supply-purchasing trips so that he and Wilma could spend a month at the MK boarding school in both the fall and the spring, not that Brazil's tropical climate changed much. It was hot year-round, and the seasons were more along the lines of dry and wet rather than any change in temperature. Still, those regular trips combined with the school breaks and long summer vacations meant that the Bowers family spent more time together during the year than they would have otherwise. Wilma was able to see that the boys were getting a good education and proper care and nurturing from like-minded missionaries. It wasn't the same as having them at home where she could enjoy their company and keep an eye on them, but as a necessity it was reassuringly good. Terry and Wilma considered themselves fortunate that God provided dorm parents who treated the children in their care like their own.

After a special evangelistic meeting in the Brazilian church in Benjamin Constant during 1975, Jim wanted to be saved. Pastor Aldenei, the local Brazilian pastor, had preached in Portuguese, in which Jim was fluent. The young boy clearly understood the sermon. Jim realized that no individual is good enough to earn God's favor because of inherent sinfulness. He knew that God, who is both holy and loving, provided a way for those He created in His own image to enjoy a relationship with Him by sacrificing His own Son, Jesus Christ, in payment for the penalty of sin.

Jim knew he had to confess his sinfulness and ask God's forgiveness, trusting that Christ's death is sufficient payment for sin, to become a Christian. He would be "born again" into a lifestyle of following God's laws instead of his own selfish desires. Terry prayed with his son that night as Jim asked Jesus to be his Savior.

Terry and Wilma didn't notice a huge change in their son after that night. Jim never had been a problem child, although they knew he was as inherently sinful as every other human being. His parents believed that the changes taking place in Jim were internal, a change of heart to conform to God's will spelled out in the Bible.

Although Jim never said, "I want to be a missionary," it was something he always thought he would do. He was certainly getting good training at his parents' side, seeing firsthand what being a missionary was all about.

Jim would look back on his childhood as an idyllic period, one of unusual freedom and exciting adventures. There were also memories that God would one day use to foster in Jim a concern for all those people in the jungle with no spiritual hope and little opportunity to hear the truth of God's Word clearly explained.

CHAPTER TWO

. . . All those who choose to follow Christ,
to suffer any loss . . .

THURSDAY, APRIL 19, 2001

The flight from Iquitos to Islandia, Peru, on Thursday, April 19, couldn't have been more perfect. The missionary group set off from the main city of Peru's Amazonas region around 7:30 A.M. upon receiving clearance from the Iquitos tower, and headed for the frontier area where Peru abuts the Amazonas regions of both Brazil and Colombia.

Pilot Kevin Donaldson, a man in his early forties, had been flying in the area for more than a dozen years and had recently finished refurbishing the single-engine Cessna floatplane in which he was flying the Bowers family. Kevin already had faxed to Lima, the capital of Peru, his written request to leave the plane overnight at Islandia, and had tried to fax his round-trip itinerary to the flight planning office at Iquitos airport just the night before. He also had called the flight planning office in Iquitos to make a verbal report of his scheduled trip. In other words, everything was going according to standard procedure.

On board OB-1408, Kevin ferried two of his missionary colleagues and their children: thirty-eight-year-old Jim Bowers, his thirty-five-year-old wife, Roni, their six-year-old son, Cory, and seven-month-old daughter, Charity, who was the whole reason behind this quick round-trip flight. The couple arranged for Kevin to fly them to the Peruvian border in order to get a permanent resident visa for Charity, the infant girl Jim and Roni had adopted in Michigan a few months earlier.

Because of the cumbersome procedure missionaries have to go through in getting residence visas—only parents receive theirs on entering the country; the children have to get theirs later—the typical procedure is to exit the country, secure a Peruvian visa at the consulate in the neighboring country, then check back in to Peru in order to fulfill all the government requirements.

Since the Bowers family lived and worked in Amazonas, Peru, where they had been missionaries with the Association of Baptists for World Evangelism since 1995, they weren't far from the border Peru shares with both Brazil and Colombia. Most residents of the three adjoining countries don't even bother with formalities such as registration, since it's not a requirement in the border region; only those needing visas pay attention to where one country ends and another begins.

Jim and Roni arranged to get Charity's visa at the Peruvian consulate in Colombia, across the Amazon River from Peru. The mission's floatplane was the obvious, logical choice for getting the Bowers family to Leticia, Colombia.

On the flight toward the Peruvian border, Jim Bowers sat in the right-hand passenger seat next to Kevin, with Cory directly behind him. Roni Bowers sat next to Cory directly behind Kevin, holding baby Charity.

The weather that Thursday was clear, with visibility for miles; only a few cotton-ball-like clouds dotted the azure skies. That's not always the case. In this tropical area, sudden storms aren't unusual, and low-lying cloud cover contributes to the humidity that is synonymous with the Amazon River and its surroundings.

A good tailwind (or possibly the newly rebuilt engine) sped the Cessna to its destination more quickly than Kevin Donaldson had expected. "It only took about an hour and forty-five minutes," he would later recall. "That's faster than I normally make the flight." Kevin's wife, Bobbi, who maintains ham-radio contact with her husband on all his flights, was able to communicate with her husband from the Donaldsons' home in Iquitos clear up to the point of his landing on the river.

Once Kevin landed at Islandia on the Yavari River, he docked OB-1408 at the floating hangar the mission maintains, under care of a local guard. They jumped into a speedboat and headed across the Amazon River to complete Charity's paperwork. Jim, Roni, and Charity trotted around to government offices that afternoon and finished their business, while Kevin played in the hotel pool with Cory.

Friends of the Bowers family back home in Michigan were just replying to letters Jim had sent the day before after finally getting e-mail service again following a three-week period when their shortwave radio e-mail connection had been inexplicably inoperable. No one—none of their friends, not Kevin, and certainly not Jim and Roni—had an inkling that the return flight to Iquitos would be anything but routine. There was no hint to any of them that perhaps this trip wasn't such a good idea after all.

If Jim Bowers's birth in Michigan was uneventful, by contrast, the birth of Veronica Lynn Luttig in Lincoln, Nebraska, on July 17, 1965, was highly dramatic. There was some question as to whether she and her mom would survive. Her parents, Garnett Luttig Sr., known as John, and Gloria, already had two boys: Garnett Jr., age five, and three-year-old Pat. With John on active duty in the U.S. Air Force, the Luttig family had lived in New Hampshire and England before being sent to Nebraska where their little girl was born.

John and Gloria met in the White Mountains of New Hampshire, where Gloria had been born and lived most of her life. John grew up in Kansas in a "dirt-poor" farming family. He joined the air force at seventeen in order to see the world and did that for four years by the time he met up with Gloria on a blind date in the fall of 1959.

Gloria's initial reluctance to be fixed up on a blind date seemed well founded when the lanky young man sporting horn-rimmed glasses and a black leather motorcycle jacket appeared at the door. After that one date, she refused to take his calls, and told her mother, "Tell him I'm not here."

John, on the other hand, was smitten with Gloria. He told a friend the day they met, "I'm gonna marry her someday." The persistent young man eventually persuaded Gloria to accept his calls, and to date him, and finally to become engaged to him. By the end of the year, they were married.

"What do you mean you 'got saved'?"

"What do you mean you 'got saved'?"

Gloria adjusted to life as an air force wife and the periods when her husband was gone for a couple of weeks at a time. She kept busy caring for her growing family. Garnett Jr., born two months prematurely in 1962, weighed only four pounds. Pat, born six months after his father was stationed in England, was completely healthy. The family lived in a renovated castle until John was reassigned back to the United States in July of 1964.

During all this time, Gloria didn't pay much attention to church other than to make sure the boys went to Sunday school every now and again. She had been raised a strict Methodist, with a grandmother who proclaimed a fire-and-brimstone fear of God, and a mother whose idea of Christianity was that anyone not born a heathen naturally was a Christian.

Gloria herself had trusted Christ for salvation at the age of twelve during a backyard summer Bible camp. She went home to share the exciting news of her conversion with her mother and grandmother. Gloria was not prepared for their response.

"What do you mean you 'got saved'?" Gloria's grandmother roared.

Her mother snorted. "You've always been a Christian! I'm not having you go back to a place where they're obviously filling your head with a lot of silly ideas."

Gloria's spiritual life all but ceased. She read her Bible from time to time, but after a succession of disappointments ending with the death of her beloved grandmother, Gloria decided she wanted nothing more to do with God.

John Luttig came from a hardworking family who didn't have time for church. As John saw it, his worst vice probably was his three-pack-a-day smoking habit. He didn't run around, he treated Gloria well, and he wasn't a bad father. He was a strict disciplinarian, sure, but other than losing his temper from time to time and the occasional drink, he couldn't see that he was such a bad guy.

The Luttigs focused on raising their family and saving John's paychecks. They didn't attend church, even on major holidays such as Christmas and Easter. They didn't perceive any need for God's help. When John was transferred back to the United States from England, the Luttigs bought a little house in Nebraska, where they began settling in and making new friends.

Roni, as John and Gloria's daughter would always be called, was conceived in the days before the existence of ultrasounds and other sophisticated medical testing that might have let the doctors know what was wrong. When Gloria was only two months pregnant with Roni, she suffered such severe nausea and vomiting that she was whisked off to the hospital to ward off dehydration. Intravenous liquids and miniscule meals throughout the day helped nourish the expectant mother, but even after being released from the hospital, Gloria continued throwing up.

When Gloria's water broke in the middle of a terrible thunderstorm, John knew he had to get her immediately to the hospital in downtown Lincoln. Not only was Gloria throwing up, as usual, but she also had started hemorrhaging.

Gloria wasn't having any contractions when she was admitted to Bryan Memorial Hospital, but Dr. Thirstein was concerned about her blood loss. He went out to the waiting room and told John, "We're going to do a Caesarean section."

Less than five minutes later, Gloria began giving birth. The placenta was breaking up, probably the cause of all Gloria's troubles for the past seven months. For a few frenzied moments, it looked as if both mother and baby might die on the spot.

Once it was clear that both Gloria and her infant daughter would survive, John was given the news that he had a six-pound-seven-ounce baby girl. Gloria, still semicomatose, was lucid enough to instruct John, "Go out and buy the prettiest little dress you can find."

John willingly complied. He found a pink dress that seemed perfect for the tiny little dark-haired girl he'd call "Gidget" or "Tater-nose" for the rest of her life. He would say later, "I believe with all my heart that when Roni was born, God lit up because He knew: This is going to be My little missionary."

Roni's dramatic birth and the medical trauma surrounding it were a harbinger of things to come. Right from birth, it was obvious that Roni suffered severe stomach problems. Her colicky screams kept her parents pacing the floor in turns with their little girl, trying to pacify her and get her to sleep. John worked long hours at the base, and Gloria still had two young boys to care for and the housework to do; both of them were so exhausted they feared losing their sanity.

Gloria took her daughter to a series of pediatricians to figure out what was wrong. The doctors were baffled. They changed Roni's formula seven times, hoping each time to find the successful solution for the baby's upset stomach. One night, while feeding Roni, Gloria could feel the formula going right through her. She called the doctor, who urged, "Get her here to the hospital as quick as you can!"

"But how?" Gloria asked. "John is away, and I have two small children."

"Call a cab if you have to," the doctor replied.

Gloria rushed to the hospital in a taxi. The doctors discovered Roni was allergic to all milk products and put the baby girl on a newly developed substance called Nutramagen. Only one drugstore in the entire city of Lincoln carried it. It was expensive—a whopping $2.19 per pound at a time when a whole loaf of bread cost only twenty-five cents—but it was worth every penny to the Luttigs to see their daughter finally begin to thrive.

Gloria didn't mind mixing the foul-smelling stuff in her blender and then straining it. She didn't even mind boiling the bottles, nipples, covers, and caps to feed it to Roni. Both John and Gloria doted on their dainty daughter, who showed the Sioux heritage of Roni's grandmother in her dusky complexion, dark hair, and brown eyes.

Roni would later be characterized as a "daddy's girl."

Roni's bout with allergies wasn't anywhere near an end. For a long time, she couldn't eat yellow vegetables of any kind. Then the family accidentally learned of Roni's medical allergies when she turned bright red after being given a penicillin shot at the doctor's office. Back they went to the doctor, who told an anxious Gloria, "Don't you ever let anyone give her penicillin again!"

Somewhere near the end of that harried year, John learned that his base was closing. The missile sites were being dismantled, and before long he wouldn't have a job. Once the base closure in Lincoln was completed, the Luttigs moved briefly to North Dakota.

They had lived there less than a year when John was called up to serve in Vietnam. With just one week of warning, Gloria took Garnett out of school, packed up and cleaned the house, shipped their goods to the East Coast, and bought train tickets to New Hampshire where she and the children would live near her mother during John's tour in Vietnam.

John kept in contact with his wife and children by tape recording messages that he sent home or phoning via the Watts ham radio in Da Nang. There was always a long line of servicemen waiting to call home, so John never knew when he'd be able to call. If his turn rolled around at two or three in the morning, then that's when he and Gloria talked.

The family's separation ended on July 5, 1968, exactly one year and one day from the date John shipped out. The boys remembered their dad, but Roni wanted nothing to do with this stranger. She didn't particularly want him hanging around her mom, either. Gradually, as John lavished affection on his children and Roni realized Gloria had plenty of love to go around, Roni warmed up to her dad. Roni would later be characterized as a "daddy's girl." And her father, while declaring his undying devotion to all his children, would admit, "Fathers have a special place in their hearts for their baby daughters."

After Vietnam, John was assigned to a base in New Jersey. Roni's new best friend was Annette, another air force "brat" with whom she made mud pies out in the backyard, "baking" them in the play kitchen stove that was part of Gloria's attempts to make Roni into a little girl. But just as Roni refused to dress in frills, so, too, the kitchen set—like the little girl who owned it—was covered from top to bottom in dirt. She and Annette went on little picnics that invariably took place in the fenced-in backyard where John had set up a swing set. Roni would hang upside down on the backyard jungle gym, swinging back and forth and scaring her mom half to death.

Although she preferred spending time in the great outdoors, Roni wasn't all tomboy. She didn't like creepy crawlies. The sight of something slithering in the grass sent her dashing indoors, screaming about "sneaky snakes."

The Luttigs spent less than three years in New Jersey before the United States Air Force transferred John yet again, this time to Hickham Air Force Base in Hawaii. The family flew across the country and the Pacific Ocean to Oahu. Roni hadn't quite finished kindergarten when the Luttig family left New Jersey. She never seemed to miss that lost month of school; it wasn't the only time she'd finish early.

A preschool physical in Hawaii before Roni started first grade revealed that she had a condition known as a "lazy eye." Both she and Garnett, also diagnosed with the condition, had to follow an intensive regimen of eye exercises. Morning, afternoon, and evening, Roni tracked the motion of a ball suspended from the ceiling by a string. A record book noted how many times a day she did each exercise.

Because Roni couldn't see out of that lazy eye, she had to wear a patch over her right eye for a while to strengthen her left eye and force it to work. With the indomitable spirit that would become her trademark, Roni stared right back at people in the stores who gaped with obvious curiosity at the child in her thick glasses and eye patch.

Other corrective measures meant Roni had to wear hard contact lenses to control the bulging of her cornea, as well as the thick glasses. The contacts had to be kept moist, something Gloria repeatedly reminded her daughter. If one popped out on the school playground, Roni licked it and stuck it right back in.

Despite her physical challenges, Roni loved to play team sports. She bowled on a junior league and joined the Green Devils, a local softball team, playing to win—another Roni trademark. When she wasn't at one of her own games, she was watching her older brothers at their baseball games.

Roni's fierce sense of competition wasn't limited to outdoor sports or organized games. Her closest friend in Hawaii was a little boy across the street who was as big a Monopoly fiend as she was. The two of them played for hours on end, sometimes starting on Saturday morning before anyone else had awakened. Gloria would come downstairs to find the two kids hard at it.

It was in Hawaii that Roni learned to swim. The five-year-old jumped from the high dive into her father's outstretched arms, and swam clear down to the bottom of the pool to pick up pennies. She'd come up, showing off her spoils and gasping, "I got it! I got it!"

Roni learned how to snorkel, too, and could keep up with her dad and brothers on ten-mile hikes. On one memorable vacation, the family literally stumbled across Waimea Canyon in Koke'e State Park on the island of Kauai. They peered into the spectacular gorge known as "the Grand Canyon of the Pacific." The natural formation boasted all manner of exotic flora and fauna that so impressed the Luttigs, they were still talking about it almost thirty years later.

The months that the Luttigs lived off base in Hawaii allowed Roni to indulge her love of animals. In addition to the family's AKC-registered miniature chocolate poodle, Pompy (short for Pompidou V), Roni won a rabbit from a local radio station one Easter and added Thumper to her little menagerie.

The minute she got home from school, Roni ran out and sat on the back step, Thumper on his leash on one side of her and Pompy on the other. She'd alternate bites of carrot between the rabbit and poodle. Thumper was known to get impatient and nibble Roni's clothing instead.

When housing became available on the air force base and the Luttigs moved there, Gloria told Roni, "Thumper is a young man who needs a wife and children of his own. He needs to live somewhere there's a lady rabbit he can marry." Roni readily released Thumper to new owners. All through her life she would be concerned about families, wanting one of her own more than almost anything else.

With two older brothers as her constant companions through all the family's moves, it's not surprising that Roni grew up something of a tomboy. She never had been crazy about dolls, although she and Pat played with his G.I. Joe action figures. Basically, anything her older brothers did, Roni wanted to do, too. For Christmas one year, Roni's dearest wish (which was granted) was for a football helmet and shoulder pads so she could play with Garnett and Pat in their neighborhood pickup games.

Working hard, playing hard, and enjoying Hawaii's incredible scenery summed up the Luttigs' tropical interlude. The Luttigs' next move, however, would have the greatest impact on their lives of any place they had ever lived. They would be changed forever, and Roni would embark on the life's course from which she never looked back.

Chapter Three

. . . And though their journey led them through the shadowlands of death . . .

5:30 A.M., FRIDAY, APRIL 20, 2001

The group of missionaries got up around 5:30 A.M. on Friday morning, April 20, in order to make the trip home to Iquitos. Because everything was so rushed, Jim and Roni didn't have time for the regular Bible reading and prayer they shared together each morning. Instead, Jim went out on the streets to find something for breakfast, settling on coffee and bread and butter that he was able to find at one of the local vendors' stands, already open at that time of the morning.

They ate quickly beside the hotel pool, pausing briefly for Jim to take pictures of Cory next to the pool. He would later wonder aloud, "Why didn't I take pictures of Roni and Charity, too? They were standing right next to me."

7:30 A.M., FRIDAY, APRIL 20, 2001

The missionaries rode a speedboat "taxi" across the river to Santa Rosa to check back in to Peru, fulfilling the final requirement for Charity's visa. Just then, Jim discovered he still had the hotel's room key in his pocket. He returned the key before rejoining his family. Then they all rode in yet another speedboat to the airplane hangar. Jim cradled Charity in his arms as she slept, and chatted with Roni during that thirty-minute boat ride.

He hopped out at the main port in the small Brazilian town where he grew up in order to do some last-minute food shopping while the others rode on to the hangar. After buying the *farinha* (a grain made from manioc root) he had loved since childhood days, Jim reached the hangar to find Roni and Kevin waiting impatiently.

Kevin asked, "What took you so long?"

The pilot had been keeping his eye on clouds beginning to roll in as the wind picked up. He worried that if Jim's shopping delayed them much longer, they might get caught in one of the sudden squalls that crop up in the region.

APPROXIMATELY 9:30 A.M., APRIL 20, 2001

Without further discussion, Jim climbed up into the seat next to Kevin. Cory sat behind him and Roni sat next to Cory, as they had done on the flight up from Iquitos. Kevin taxied out into the Yavari River and took off, flying low enough to stay below the clouds that had blown in and visually maintain reference to the serpentine Amazon River which serves as the border between Peru and Brazil.

The passengers on OB-1408 had no reason to suspect that within minutes of their takeoff, a surveillance plane operated by employees of the U.S. Central Intelligence Agency noted their presence. As the Citation jet that monitored possible drug traffickers tracked the Cessna, the CIA employees alerted their Peruvian liaison on board the Citation. He then contacted the Peruvian air force in order to check out the identity and intentions of the floatplane.

Under the legislation enacted by the U.S. Congress in 1994, the president of the United States was authorized to make determinations that would allow United States personnel to provide assistance to countries taking action against civilian aircraft if: 1) the president determined that the drug trafficking posed an extraordinary threat to the national security of that country, and 2) the country had "appropriate procedures in place to protect against the innocent loss of life, . . . which shall at a minimum include effective means to identify and warn an aircraft before the use of force directed against the aircraft."[1]

President Clinton made those determinations with respect to Peruvian drug flight interdiction in December 1994. The United States government agencies participating in this drug interdiction effort since that time included the CIA, Department of Defense, Customs Service, and members of the United States Coast Guard, Navy, and Air Force.

Under the program as approved by President Clinton, Peru had established a detailed list of procedures to be followed in ensuring against the loss of innocent life. The list provided four phases of Peru's air interdiction program: detection, identification, interception, and use of weapons.[2]

The first phase—detection—involved the United States and Peruvian authorities detecting and monitoring any aircraft passing through the high drug trafficking zone of the Amazon region. This was done both on the ground with sophisticated radar systems operated by the United States Department of Defense, and in the air, mainly through CIA-operated surveillance aircraft.

The identification phase—phase two—involved attempting to determine the identity of a suspect airplane from the ground or via surveillance aircraft. It was to include determining whether the suspect aircraft was on a previously filed flight plan and attempting to establish radio contact with that aircraft.

During phase three, if it was not possible to verify a flight plan or to establish communication and identify the aircraft as innocent, the commanding general (or, in his absence, his chief of staff) of the Peruvian Air Force Sixth Territorial Region (the

Amazon region) could authorize launch of an interceptor aircraft "to visually identify the aircraft, verify its registry, and attempt to establish radio contact, and, if necessary, cause the aircraft to proceed to a safe and adequate air strip . . . using procedures consistent with International Civil Aviation Organization guidelines."

The procedures approved by President Clinton reinforced that, if radio contact was not possible, the interceptor pilot "must use a series of internationally recognized procedures to make visual contact with the suspect aircraft, and to direct the aircraft to follow the intercepting aircraft to a secure airfield for inspection." ICAO guidelines specify in that situation that an interceptor should circle around the suspect aircraft several times, pulling ahead and to the left-hand (pilot's) side and waggling its wings and turning its lights off and on, signifying "follow me," and then moving off at a slight angle to the left.

The final phase—use of weapons—was to go into effect only if the suspect aircraft continued "to ignore the internationally recognized instructions to land." The interceptor pilot, after receiving permission from the commanding general, could fire warning shots. If those were ignored, and "only after again obtaining the approval of the commanding general," the interceptor pilot could fire to disable an airplane. Finally, if such fire did not cause the intercepted pilot to obey air force instructions to land, the commanding general could authorize fire to shoot down the suspect aircraft.

Unbeknownst to the rest of the world, however, the procedures to protect against the loss of innocent life upon which the program had been approved in 1994 had eroded considerably by 2001. There were no longer four phases, only three. Many of the steps within each phase had been abbreviated or disappeared altogether. And there was no memory of the way things should have been done, because the United States and Peruvian personnel participating directly in the interception process rotated through the program, known as "air bridge denial," on a frequent basis.[3]

In April of 2001, when the CIA alerted their Peruvian liaison about the presence of OB-1408 and he, in turn, contacted his country's air force, they unleashed a chain of events that gathered force like a runaway train.

While Roni and her family hopped around the United States wherever her dad's job took them, Jim Bowers and his family had a well-established routine of shuttling between Brazil and Michigan. The Bowers family's third furlough from the Amazon region started during the United States's bicentennial celebrations.

Accustomed to being given significant amounts of responsibility, such as helping to construct school buildings or teach Sunday school classes, the Bowers boys marveled at peers who lived with very little responsibility or experience of the world.

But once they got acclimated and were able to avoid the major pitfalls that loomed for an innocent "jungle bunny" at the Baptist Academy in Grand Rapids, Michigan, the Bowers brothers settled in happily to life in the United States. They were used to playing soccer Brazilian style, but they were introduced to a new game, baseball. Family friend Jim Kramer recalls first meeting the brothers on a visit when all they wanted to do was play baseball. "I was tired after a couple of hours," he said, "but they just kept on going."

Terry traveled to the churches who pledged money to the Bowers family, telling about the activities of the past four years. He explained that his aviation work not only helped other missionaries by ferrying supplies to them, but also aided in spreading the gospel to otherwise inaccessible areas. Either Terry himself preached in those remote places or, as was increasingly the case, he took young Brazilian pastors to preach and to teach the new Christians. People were being saved and churches started in Amazonian settlements and towns where the gospel had never been preached before. Terry found it exciting and fulfilling, because he understood the eternal significance of his work.

Wilma and the three boys traveled with Terry to churches as their schedule permitted, but with school and extracurricular activities, they weren't able to accompany him as often as they would have liked. Most women wanted to know what it was like raising children in what they perceived to be the "fearsome" Amazon region. Wilma corrected their misconceptions, telling them, "It's much like raising children here in the United States." Her location might have been slightly more exotic, but her main concerns, too, were raising her children to love and follow God, and to become well-behaved and well-rounded individuals.

The Bowers family returned to Brazil in 1977; the three boys to the New Tribes Mission boarding school, Puraquequara, their parents to home base in Benjamin Constant and their ministry in the Baptist church there and the new churches being started along the river.

By his own admission, Jim wasn't much of a student. He hated to read, which meant all of his schooling suffered as a result. Book reports were the worst; trying to read a book within the allotted time frame, much less remember it and explain what it was about, was the last thing he wanted to do. He managed to keep up with his work sufficiently to be allowed to participate in sports, band, chorale, and other privileges outside the classroom. He would look back on these years as a happy and fun time, despite the huge difficulty posed by having to live away from home for more than eight months out of each year.

Wilma noticed that her boys came home from Puraquequara with a wide variety of skills. They were able to read music, play an instrument, compete fairly, build simple structures, and dismantle and repair engines. They even learned how to drive on the boarding school's old tractor.

Each time Wilma packed their suitcases, though, she wept and wondered, *What am I doing?* She knew that it wasn't in anyone's best interest to let her boys wander the streets of Benjamin Constant, and she reminded herself that the difficult separation benefited her boys in ways beyond her capabilities at home. Those twice-yearly supply flights to the school in Terry's airplane helped ease her loneliness a little.

The highlight of Wilma's year was the boys' Christmas break. As choir director and youth leader at the church in Benjamin Constant, she made sure that Phil, Jim, and Dan took part in the annual Christmas program, memorizing lines for the play or music for the cantata. The church celebration took place on the Sunday closest to Christmas or on Christmas Day itself.

Once Jim got an idea in his head,
he steadily worked toward achieving his goal.

With her own special memories of Christmas at home in Michigan, Wilma was determined that her boys would grow up with fond memories of the season, too. She developed Bowers family traditions that included her sons. One of them took place on Christmas Eve when the Brazilians who helped Wilma and Terry brought their families to the Bowers house for a communal Christmas dinner. The meal was followed by singing Christmas carols and reading the account of Christ's birth from Luke 2.

Presents for their friends were piled high and deep under the tree: giant washbasins for the women to do their laundry in, material from which to make clothes, enough food for each family to eat a big meal, and other practical items, as well as toys for each of the children. It was the Bowers boys' responsibility to pass out the gifts, a duty they relished.

Once that feat had been accomplished, the area under the tree was nearly bare. Few packages remained for the Bowers family, although some had been deliberately held back so as not to overwhelm the Brazilians. Still, the emphasis was on giving, not on getting. It was a lesson all three boys would carry with them into adulthood.

During the school year, Jim and his brothers participated in the teen services at Puraquequara by ushering, singing special music, and occasionally helping to lead the service. Jim still hadn't articulated to anyone a specific desire for a career in missions, but he was headed in that direction, already showing signs of the trait that would characterize him as an adult. Wilma and Terry noticed that once Jim got an idea in his head, he steadily worked toward achieving his goal.

Jim spent his final year of high school living with his parents in the home they bought in Michigan and rented out between furloughs. He attended Grand Rapids Baptist Academy, rejoining the same group of kids he'd spent eighth grade with, so the cultural adjustments weren't as great as if he'd gone into a group of total strangers, although it took a little time to get used to the United States again.

First of all, everything was much more formal than what Jim was used to at the MK boarding school in Brazil. Dress codes were far stricter at the academy than at Puraquequara. It wasn't acceptable to appear in class wearing shorts and flip-flops, and setting out across town on dark, cold Michigan winter mornings was quite different from the tropical heat of Brazil.

On the other hand, he had been sheltered from a great deal. Unlike kids in the United States—even kids in Christian school and in the Bowers family's home church—he hadn't paid attention to things like current events, fashion trends, and what was popular in music. He hadn't seen a television for four years, not even shows such as *Gilligan's Island, Hogan's Heroes,* and *Star Trek.*

Although he made friends easily enough and had his younger brother, Dan, there, too, Jim felt somewhat out of place during his senior year. It certainly wasn't apparent to most people. Jim's job at a local pizza shop made him responsible enough to be able to buy his first car, a used Camaro. And Jim must have impressed his boss as being trustworthy, because Jim not only drove himself to school but also picked up his boss's two daughters on the way to school.

"That's the last thing I would have done," Jim later remarked. "Have a boy straight from the jungle, just starting to drive—in the winter, in Michigan—going by his house every morning to take his daughters to school." Jim drove to school and delivered pizzas all through that first Michigan winter. His training on the old tractor at Puraquequara must have done something right since he never had an accident.

Jim's senior year wasn't all work. He played on the Baptist Academy soccer team, in the school band, and was involved in teen ministries at church. He was quickly learning what life was like for a teenager in the United States. Although he felt awkward, Jim didn't particularly want to feel too comfortable with some of what he observed. Some of the kids in his school began drinking when their parents weren't home. That wasn't anything Jim wanted in his life. He tried to steer clear of a wild lifestyle that would dishonor God and his parents and might keep him from achieving his goal of a career in missions.

Terry was diagnosed with polycystic kidney disease and was advised by his doctors not to continue working in the tropical Amazon River region. He received permission from ABWE and from the family's supporters to spend an extra year in the States, teaching at the missionary aviation school that was part of Piedmont Bible College. Because Terry's health hadn't been good, he and Wilma asked Jim if he'd live at home with them during his first year of college.

The Bowers family relocated to Winston-Salem, and Jim enrolled in Piedmont Bible College. He planned to become a missionary pilot like his dad and spent the first year of the five-year aviation course studying for his aircraft mechanic's license.

During his first year at college, Jim developed friendships with a bunch of other MKs, many of whom also played soccer and had grown up in Brazil or one of the African countries. Because the Bible college was small—only about 550 students—it wasn't overwhelming to him. Jim got as involved as possible on campus and at church and worked a few different jobs as he became more accustomed to life in the United States.

When Terry and Wilma returned to Brazil in the summer of 1982 to work in the more temperate climate of southern Brazil, Jim was studying through the summer to complete his aircraft maintenance training. Then he moved onto the PBC campus for the fall semester.

Roni's zeal for missions was evident.

During the second month of his second year of college, Jim took special notice of a certain new girl on campus, Roni Luttig. He asked the sixteen-year-old freshman to join him and some of his friends to get ice cream and go roller skating. Jim didn't consider the two of them a couple for quite a long time, although Roni did take him home at Thanksgiving. They both went out with other people that year, insisting that they were just friends.

Jim sent Roni's picture to his parents, telling them a little bit about the girl he was taking to the school banquet. As his mother recalls, Jim wanted them to know that he'd met a girl who was special, but he assured them that this wasn't a serious relationship.

In the spring of 1983, things began to change. Wilma and Terry were getting letters and phone calls filled with "Roni and I" this, "Roni and I" that. Jim and Roni went to her parents' in Virginia almost every weekend, a five-hour ride on Jim's motorcycle. They ate breakfast and lunch together in the school cafeteria, had classes together, went to work at Hechinger's together after school, then returned to campus and studied together.

They were still claiming to be just friends—good friends —but the only people they were fooling were themselves.

Jim planned to go home to Brazil over Christmas that year and asked Roni if she wanted to go along. He didn't have any conscious thought of this being a significant introduction to his parents or a precursor to engagement. He thought of Roni as a good friend and someone who certainly could figure in his future. When Roni said that she'd like to go, Jim asked the permission of PBC's dean of women for Roni to accompany him. It was nothing short of miraculous to the two students that Dean Hartwig, a former ABWE missionary to Brazil, agreed.

"At a Bible college where underclassmen were not supposed to go down the road together without a chaperone," Jim recalled, "they let us go to Brazil, flying all the way down there and staying with friends in Miami and Bogotá [Colombia], too."

That three-week visit to Brazil solidified the "just-friendship." The striking, energetic teenager their son brought down for Christmas endeared herself to Wilma by entering in to whatever was going on, whether it was helping prepare meals, decorating for the holidays, or playing games. She appeared to have no reservations about fitting into the jungle surroundings and way of life.

If this is what God wants, the missionary mother thought to herself, *my son is going to have an excellent wife.* Roni's zeal for missions was evident; she had traveled extensively and was obviously well-educated. Wilma could see in her the makings of a well-rounded, well-qualified missionary wife. She and Terry thoroughly approved of Roni.

Dan was still living at home, and Phil had traveled down for the Christmas holidays, so both brothers were able to meet and vet Jim's girlfriend. They found Roni eager to join in any activity, although they thought she was a little fainthearted. There was the infamous shower incident when her panicked shrieking brought everyone racing to the bathroom to find out what was the matter.

"Get it!" Roni's voice squealed through the locked door. "Get it!"

Once Roni was decent and made a speedy exit, the brave brothers rushed in to find . . . a tree frog, its bright green, shiny back hopping all over the shower stall and its little suction feet sticking to the walls.

As time passed and their friendship grew, it became apparent to Jim and Roni that God had brought them together and that marriage was a good possibility. They both were focused on finishing school, both headed toward missions careers, and both active in a church near Piedmont Bible College where they sang in the choir and taught Sunday school.

Jim had decided to leave the flight training portion of the missionary aviation program for his final year at Piedmont. That way, he could concentrate on nothing but flying and have all his other course work out of the way. And, too, by then he might be able to afford the $12,000 or so that flying would cost him just for that final year of pilot training.

CHAPTER FOUR

. . . The song of their commitment
they rehearsed with every breath. . .

10:00 A.M., APRIL 20, 2001

One of the American CIA pilots asked the Peruvian liaison, "Are we launching the A-37s? Has that happened yet?"[1]

"Yes," the liaison responded.

Ten minutes later, the same pilot repeated what he understood to be the procedures. ". . . I think when the A-37s get here, we are going to do phase one, correct?"

The Peruvian replied in the affirmative.

The American reiterated, "I don't know if this is *bandito* or it's *amigo,* OK? I don't know. It's possible we'll get him to land in Iquitos and check, OK? Before. . ." and the pilot made machine-gun-like noises before concluding, "you know?"

"Yes, yes. Very good," the Peruvian approved.

But it was only minutes later that the CIA pilot interrupted his Peruvian liaison's radio transmissions to say, "It doesn't match the [drug trafficker] profile. He's flying too high."

He repeated his observation a few minutes later, saying, "He's flying at the proper hemispheric altitude [for a nondrug flight]."

10:35 A.M., APRIL 20, 2001

The Americans on board the CIA's observation aircraft could hear their Peruvian liaison talking to the Peruvian air force pilots in the A-37. After several failed attempts to make radio contact with OB-1408, the liaison told his air force's pilots, "We've gone ahead with phase one and are now going to proceed with phase two. Do you copy?"

The Americans repeated their observation that the Cessna "doesn't fit the profile," adding, "We don't want to do it. Hold it!" One of the pilots radioed the United States officer on the ground, whose office was right next to that of the Peruvian officer in command of the interdiction mission. The Peruvian and American officers communicated with their respective personnel by radio, and the Peruvian liaison on the Citation was also able to make radio contact with his country's air force.

When the pilot onboard the CIA Citation reported to his officer, he said, "I understand it's not our call, but this guy is at 4,500 feet and he is not taking any evasive action. I recommend we follow him but do not recommend phase three at this time."

The American officer asked, "Has the host nation been in touch with [the airplane in question]?"

"No."[2]

It would later be learned that the Peruvian air force had contacted the tower in Iquitos to report that they were tracking a floatplane and to ask the whereabouts of OB-1408.

OB-1408, which Kevin was flying, was registered to the Asociacion Bautista para Evangelismo Mundial (ABEM), the organization under which ABWE missionaries work in Peru and is one of only two private floatplanes regularly operating out of Iquitos.

While Jim's teen years were spent in the nearly idyllic setting of Puraquequara, Roni's adolescence in Virginia had few bright spots. The biggest of them came when her dad retired from the air force in 1975. The Luttigs settled in Poquoson, Virginia, on the eastern coast near Newport News and Hampton. The pastor of a local church came to welcome the new residents to town.

As soon as the minister arrived at the front door, John was out the back. He was sure the pastor was going to complain about his smoking habit; after all, Garnett refused even to touch the things when John said, "Bring me my cigarettes." Garnett knew better than to disobey his dad, but he'd either wrap the pack in a towel or pull down his shirt sleeves to cover his hands so he didn't have to touch the cigarettes.

John also figured the preacher wanted money, a notion he had of every preacher. He thought, *If this guy wants money, why doesn't he go get himself a job? I work; I feed my family. Why can't he?* Suspicion piled on resentment did little to foster John's amiability toward the preacher.

Gloria, however, had tired of running from God. When the Baptist pastor continued calling on the Luttig family, Gloria admitted that she had done her family a great injustice by not making sure they heard and understood the gospel message. What if they died without accepting Christ as their personal Savior? Her future was secure, but what eternal consequences for her family might result from Gloria's negligence?

The pastor's persistence paid off. Between July and November of that year, not only had Gloria returned to her relationship with God, but the rest of her family had prayed to receive Christ as Savior. After John was saved on November 22, the entire family was baptized.

The salvation of the Luttigs created major changes in the family's life. For one thing, they all got involved in their local Baptist church, attending every service. Garnett and Pat joined the teen group; Gloria sang solos; John became a deacon. Not only were they all active in the church, but things at home changed, too. John no longer smoked cigarettes, and he worked at keeping his flash-point temper under control. Gloria faithfully read her Bible and taught scriptural principles to her children.

After her salvation, Roni determined that she was going to be a missionary and announced her decision to her parents. Gloria thought, *That's not bad. Last year she wanted to be a veterinarian, and a year from now she may decide to become a politician, but a missionary is certainly an admirable aspiration.* But Roni never second-guessed her decision. Once she set her eyes on a career in missions, everything she did—or didn't do—was determined in light of that goal. As time passed, Roni grew more convinced that God was leading her into foreign missionary service.

The Luttigs often had missionaries eat a meal in their home or stay overnight. From them, Roni learned everything she could about missionary life. Like a sponge, she soaked up the adults' conversation and interjected a few of her own questions. It seemed as if she were cramming for a test, filing away the missionaries' answers for a later day.

One of the less bright spots in Roni's life at the time was another food allergy. The family ate fish sticks at least twice a month for dinner. By 1:00 A.M. after one of those meals, Roni was overcome with violent vomiting and diarrhea. That meant more trips to the doctor. This time the diagnosis was that Roni had become allergic to iodine and fish of all kinds. Gloria had outgrown her own early allergies to milk and some shellfish, but Roni never did. She would always have to be careful about what she ate.

In junior high school, Roni kept up with her softball. At a game that is still clear in a proud father's memory, one of the opponents hit the ball to right field where Roni caught it, threw it to first base, and struck out the runner before she ever got there.

With her two older brothers in the church senior high youth group, Roni begged to be allowed into the ProTeens program a little bit early. "I know all the verses as well as the older kids," she argued.

But Bill Flowers, the youth pastor, adamantly refused. He said, "You wait until each stage. If you start now, what will you do when you're in high school? And what about other kids who might want to join early? Where do we draw the line?"

It galled Roni to be kept out of an activity by something as trivial as age. Pat, the brother nearest her age, was always just a little bit ahead of her. He started dating before she did and could drive a car earlier. The "me, too" little sister who'd suited up to play in their casual football games now sat on the sidelines.

Roni maintained her lifelong devotion to animals, raising chickens and a guinea pig that she fed with an eyedropper. The family had another poodle by this time, Little Bit, and Roni brought home a cat she named Neptune. It wasn't long after she got Neptune that the family was kept from attending a Wednesday evening church service when Pat found Neptune under a bed, delivering kittens.

Roni's closest friends were her family members.

It turned out that Garnett and Roni were allergic to cats. After the siblings had sneezed one time too many, Gloria issued an ultimatum: "The cat has got to go." Roni was miserable enough that she agreed. The two allergy sufferers loaded the cat—kittens and all—into Garnett's brand-new Ford Pinto and drove off to the animal shelter. By the time they arrived after being confined in close quarters with the cats, their eyes were streaming.

"Obviously, the lady thought we were both really sad about giving up the cats," Garnett said. He must have broken her heart when he handed her a dollar to take the cats off their hands.

When she entered high school, Roni's dearest wish was to join the drill team. She didn't want to be a cheerleader, but she longed to carry a flag and do the precision maneuvers. She wasn't chosen to participate, a regret that echoed many earlier disappointments.

Like many teenagers, Roni battled acne for a couple of years, but she didn't let it inhibit her any more than the eye patch in Hawaii had. Her brilliant smile, something Pastor White once commented on from the pulpit at Central Baptist Church to Roni's everlasting embarrassment, is something friends and acquaintances still recall. And she had the vibrant personality to go along with her joy-filled smile.

Behind that smile lay a smart and dedicated student. Roni received excellent grades because she applied the same intensity to her studies that she did to everything she tackled. That intensity could be intimidating, especially to other teenage girls who weren't quite so certain of their futures as Roni seemed to be about hers.

Roni wasn't interested in just hanging out at the malls and talking about boys. She had plenty to do with her job at a local craft store, counseling at Camp Open Arms every summer, and putting extra effort into her schoolwork. It was undoubtedly that single-minded focus that made Roni throw herself down onto the bed and burst into tears. "I don't have any real friends!" she sobbed to Gloria.

"What do you mean?" her mother asked. Roni always seemed to be talking to people at church, and Bill and Sue Flowers, the youth leaders, counted Roni as one of the dependable members of their group.

"The other girls don't understand me, and I don't want to be like them," Roni said. She didn't get involved in many of the activities others at Poquoson High did. She wouldn't join them in drinking and dancing; she wasn't promiscuous. "She simply didn't want to do anything that might bring harm to her testimony, dishonor God, or prevent her from becoming a missionary," Roni's mother would say years later. "She wanted to remain pure."

Roni's closest friends were her family members. She watched football with her dad and older brothers, rooting for the Nebraska Cornhuskers with the male Luttigs but cheering on the Dallas Cowboys against their favorite NFL teams. She confided in her mom, someone who understood her devotion to missions and didn't try to make her into someone she wasn't. Not that the two never disagreed.

One night, Roni came home and announced that she had decided to attend a Christian rock concert.

Gloria fired back, "I don't think so, Roni!"

"But my friends are going," Roni protested.

Her mother refused to budge. "Honey, I don't care who's going; you're not."

Gloria's tone brooked no quarrel. Roni said, through her tears, "You're my mother so I have to do what you say, but I don't always understand."

The teenager was no Goody Two-shoes who never had a light moment. Roni had always loved to laugh; she appreciated a joke even if—or maybe especially when—it was on her. She listened to music by the Carpenters, the Beach Boys, and Chicago, as well as the contemporary Christian vocal artists such as Sandi Patti, Keith Green, and others. She and her mom sang duets together at church, sometimes accompanied on the guitar by Garnett.

Gloria was in charge of many of the dramatic productions at Grace Baptist Church, so Roni was used to helping out around the set. When Pat had the leading role in one of the productions, Roni coached her brother on his part, making sure he knew his lines. But due to Pat's illness on opening night—more nerves than anything, his mother guessed—Roni took his place. She'd memorized all the parts and had no trouble performing in public.

Roni was a girls' counselor at Camp Open Arms, the same

Christian summer camp where Garnett worked as a lifeguard and her mom cooked. Part of Roni's responsibilities included teaching lessons and crafts, although she also played with the girls and was plenty of fun, according to one of the girls who remembered her teen counselor.

Roni had two boyfriends in high school (one would go on to become a youth pastor; the other would excel in an air force career), but since she was so young and neither of the men professed an interest in missions, the relationships never became serious.

When it was time for her junior year of high school, Roni asked her parents to let her skip right on to her senior year. By this time, Garnett and Pat had joined the Marine Corps, and school was now just a drudgery to be endured each day. Roni was eager to start college and move forward in her pursuit of a missionary career. John and Gloria gave their permission, which meant that Roni graduated from high school at the age of sixteen.

Her commencement ceremony wasn't memorable for that reason alone. Roni had severely sprained her ankle just a few days earlier and wasn't able to march across the platform to receive her diploma. Instead she hobbled up to the base of the platform on crutches. A picture of the event shows Roni rolling her eyes in self-deprecation as if to ask, "Can you believe this?"

At Garnett's wedding a few days later, Roni slathered her swollen foot with numbing sports spray in order to walk down the aisle without crutches or a cane. She seemed determined not to let anything get in the way of whatever she had set her mind to do, whether it was being a bridesmaid "just like everyone else" or becoming a missionary. There was an impatience about Roni to get on to the next phase, whatever that was. It was a trait that would characterize her throughout her life.

Roni arrived at Piedmont Bible College as a sixteen-year-old freshman, certain of one thing: She was going to be a missionary. She took her life's vocation seriously and wasn't going to let anything sidetrack her. She told her mom before leaving home, "I'm going to marry a short, blond missionary." Gloria would have cause to recall that prediction (premonition?) years later, but at the time it seemed nothing more than a testimony to her daughter's strong convictions.

Anyone who asked Roni for a date—and there were several who noticed the vivacious girl with the striking complexion and ready smile—first had to correctly answer the question, "What do you plan to do with your life?" Only those who responded "be a missionary" were considered.

It was within her first year that Roni met Jim Bowers. "Oh, Mama, I met this boy and he's so cute! He has a motorcycle." Roni's enthusiastic description reminded Gloria of her own meeting with John some years earlier. History was repeating itself.

Roni was obviously enthralled. "He's so cute, but I don't think he even knows I'm alive."

Gloria, ever practical, suggested, "Get somebody to introduce you."

Roni said, "I think he's already dating somebody."

"Is he engaged?"

"Well, no."

As it happened, not only did Jim ask Roni out, he answered her first big question correctly—yes, he was serious about becoming a missionary—and the two went out for ice cream and roller skating.

When Roni took Jim home to meet her parents that Thanksgiving, Gloria had already been primed by Roni's calls home. She and John decided Jim was polite and pleasant, but since both he and Roni were still so young, they didn't view the teenagers as a serious couple.

Garnett was pleasantly surprised with his little sister's choice for a boyfriend. He had heard she was dating a prospective missionary, and he imagined a stuffy, serious man, not a laid-back person who obviously had a sense of fun and rode a motorcycle. Nobody was asking for his blessing, but Garnett thought Jim wasn't half bad; in fact, he would probably say his sister's boyfriend (although Jim would never have called himself that) was OK by him.

A verse in Proverbs says, "As iron sharpens iron, so one man sharpens another" (27:17). That's what Jim and Roni did for each other. Roni's fiercely competitive streak struck a resounding chord in the normally easygoing Jim. In their studies, they vied to see who could get the better grades, an honor that almost always went to Roni.

With his more introspective and deliberate nature, Jim was quiet where Roni was outgoing and impulsive. They were both very active, willing to try almost anything, and took up strenuous activities such as climbing, diving, and skiing. Whereas Roni struggled with physical limitations and health concerns, Jim had always enjoyed great health. They both needed strong glasses (and almost always wore contacts) but other than that, Jim was as healthy as the proverbial horse.

Roni's enthusiasm and energy were contagious; she wanted to do things. If no one else had any ideas, she certainly did. Part of the attraction was that she focused on whatever she was doing, giving it everything she had. Roni was good at organizing people and getting them involved, and her distinctive laugh has been described as "infectious."

Sherie Bostic, one of Roni's roommates at Piedmont, recalls a prank the two girls pulled in the middle of the night. Roni and Sherie shared an air force background that had taken them all over the world and made it hard to form close friendships. They hit it off immediately, sharing a similar sense of fun.

Roni and Sherie set their alarms for 2:00 A.M., in order to get up when the rest of the dorm was fast asleep. One time they set off smoke alarms on different floors in the dorm. Another time they figured on some "payback" for the room directly above theirs where other girls played an electronic keyboard at high volume. Roni and Sherie crept upstairs in the dark, programmed the keyboard to come on at a certain time—at full volume, of course—and ran back up to their room to wait for the hilarity that was sure to follow.

They waited and waited—and waited—but nothing happened. They sneaked back upstairs, reset the keyboard, and snorted with laughter all the way back to their room as the keyboard switched on. Roni was a little perturbed with Sherie for turning the volume below maximum. She even wrote in Sherie's yearbook, ". . . I guess the thing I will remember most is turning the piano on. Should have kept the volume up, but that's okay."

It's a wonder they weren't found out since they were rolling on the floor of their room, laughing so hard their faces and stomachs hurt. Their scheme was exactly the kind of joke Roni liked to play on other people: mischievous but essentially harmless.

Sherie remembers Roni expressing concern for her spiritual state. "Roni always had her devotions and prayed in the morning. I could say she 'preached to me,' but it wasn't to that extent. I could tell she was concerned about me. I didn't come from the best of backgrounds."

Roni also urged Sherie to get out and do things with other kids on campus. "I didn't make friends real easy," Sherie said. Roni later wrote to her, "I really hope that you will find what you want to do through God's eyes. Keep looking at Him for guidance. I know you will."

While encouraging her college friends, Roni herself experienced more medical problems. She suffered frequent, severe stomach pains, but the doctors couldn't figure out a cause. The excruciating pains came and went; Roni never knew when they would strike. She also had to deal with a fibrocystic problem. Medical experts recommended that Roni not consume caffeine or chocolate, and have frequent checkups and mammograms to make sure none of the cysts turned cancerous. It was a concern that Roni had to learn to leave in God's hands, trusting Him to take care of her.

The major blow to Roni was that she had to learn to live without chocolate. One of her favorite foods in the whole world was Oreo cookies. "She could live on them," her brother, Pat, said. That was no exaggeration; she'd been known to eat an entire package by herself in one sitting.

Even though she faced many medical challenges, Roni's faith never wavered. She never asked God "Why me?" and didn't complain to her friends about her physical limitations. If anything, the difficulties she faced made her more determined than ever that nothing would keep her from serving God to her utmost. She found encouragement in passages such as Joshua chapter one. "Have I not commanded you? Be strong and courageous. Do not be terrified; do not be discouraged, for the LORD your God will be with you wherever you go" (1:9). The apostle Paul wrote, "One thing I do: Forgetting what is behind and straining toward what is ahead, I press on toward the goal to win the prize for which God has called me heavenward in Christ Jesus" (Philippians 3:13b–14). James 1:12 reads, "Blessed is the man who perseveres under trial, because when he has stood the test, he will receive the crown of life that God has promised to those who love him."

Jim had been planning
the proposal for quite some time.

Throughout the years that they dated, Roni was a teenager and Jim barely into his twenties. They gained valuable experience working in the AWANA program of the local church. They led the middle school children who participated in the Bible club, helped them memorize verses, and organized the strenuous games that are part of the routine. Despite that maturing, however, it wasn't likely that any mission board would take people quite as young and inexperienced as they were, a fact Roni later acknowledged to her mother.

In May of 1985, when the school year at Piedmont was drawing to a close, many of Roni's friends were showing off their engagement rings. Although she and Jim had been dating longer than most students, Roni still didn't have a ring. She began to wonder if Jim was really as serious about her as she had assumed.

Jim had been planning the proposal for quite some time. Despite frequent temptations to end all of the speculating by dragging out the ring box and thrusting it into Roni's hand with an offhand remark, Jim resisted and continued to plan "the moment."

He had bought a '65 Ford Mustang that he was trying to repair. It was an indication of how serious he and Roni were that he referred to the car as "ours." The transmission wasn't working, and Jim had gotten two other transmissions from the junkyard to salvage bits from all three in order to make one working part. Whatever free time he had, Jim spent in his dorm room, covered in grease, with the engine pieces spread on the floor around him.

On one of those days, Roni was helping Jim with his tinkering, and they got into something of an argument about the delicate issue of an engagement. Roni wondered whether Jim was as serious about her as she hoped. Perhaps he didn't want to get married, or at least, not to her. She began crying.

Jim found himself saying something like, "Wait here a minute." He went to his dresser drawer and pulled out the diamond ring. He had time to think, *I'll just have to give her the ring now and then tell her about the plan I had for the end of the school year.*

And that's what he did, covered in grease though they were. In an instant, Roni's tears of consternation turned to tears of joy. Hers was one of the most unusual engagement stories that year, and one that she would laughingly share in the coming years with anyone who asked her, "So, how did you two get engaged?"

Jim and Roni repaired the Mustang's transmission, finished their junior year at Piedmont Bible College, and drove down to Panama City, Florida, where John and Gloria Luttig had recently moved. Terry and Wilma Bowers came back to the States and met up with the newly engaged couple at the Luttigs' home. The two sets of parents and their children spent a week getting to know one another better and talking about the future. It was a memorable time for both families, and a good chance for Jim and Roni to enjoy the blessing and approval of their parents, something important to both of them.

Jim had finally figured out a way to pay for his last year of aviation training, the expensive part of the hands-on flying itself. He figured out that if he joined the United States Army, the G.I. Bill would pay for the cost of flight training.

Gloria and Wilma concluded that the military stint could be good for the young couple's marriage. The pair would have two years away from family and friends to bond as a couple and learn to become a family of their own. Terry thought it sounded like a good idea. John, who spent twenty years in the United States Air Force, also approved of the plan. He assured Terry, "It will be a good experience for Jim in many ways."

Jim left Roni (and the Mustang) with her parents and caught a bus to Fort Knox, Kentucky, to enlist. After joining up, Jim found out that things weren't quite what he had been led to expect at the recruiting office back in Michigan. But by then it was too late to turn back.

Jim wouldn't get the $15,000 G.I. Bill in a lump sum that he could use for the final year of aviation training. Instead, the army would reimburse Jim only as he could prove he was spending a certain number of hours as a full-time student. This meant that Jim would have to come up with some other way to earn or borrow the nearly $1,300 per month that flying cost.

Jim and Roni knew that God wanted the two of them on the mission field. Perhaps during their time in the army, God would reveal some way to acquire the money for Jim to finish aviation training. They couldn't see how or from where, but Jim and Roni would have to be patient and follow the next step. God would show them at the right time what He wanted them to do. They remembered verses they had memorized in childhood. Proverbs 3:5–6 said, "Trust in the LORD with all your heart and lean not on your own understanding; in all your ways acknowledge him, and he will make your paths straight." Another good admonition came from Psalm 32:8: "I will instruct you and teach you in the way you should go; I will counsel you and watch over you."

CHAPTER FIVE

. . . I will serve the Lord.
I will serve the Lord my God . . .

10:37 A.M., APRIL 20, 2001

In the front passenger seat of the Cessna, Jim Bowers snapped pictures of Caballococha, one of the many towns where the Amazon and its tributaries snake through tropical rain forest, and where tiny villages of thatched-roof huts sporadically dot the riverbank.

It had been a long time since Jim and Roni had seen the area where they worked from such a lofty vantage point. Jim sent an e-mail to a friend in Michigan just before leaving on the two-day trip. He wrote, "I'm looking forward to getting a good view of all our towns from the air again . . . I'll get a better feel for how they're situated, and their full size and location on the river."

A brief rain shower doused the little floatplane on its route to Iquitos, but it wasn't severe enough to force them to divert their course. Kevin's habit was to use GPS points (global positioning system, a geographical tracking system that bases exact locations on satellite transmission), making sure he stayed within five miles of the water so he could glide down safely if anything happened to his engine. He knows a floatplane pilot who hazards a direct route—over rain forest the entire two hours—but Kevin knows it isn't necessary to take that risk just to shave a few minutes off his flying time.

While Jim juggled his camera and baby daughter and talked to Kevin through their intercom headphones, Roni and Cory napped in the back seats. When Roni woke up, Jim passed Charity back to her so she could take another turn at cuddling their little girl.

10:45 A.M., APRIL 20, 2001

While looking at the sights down below, Jim glimpsed from the corner of his eye something in the air, behind and to the right of the Cessna. It was a fighter plane from the Peruvian air force. Jim asked Roni to wake up Cory. "He'll want to see this." Cory was as enthusiastic about planes as Jim had been at his age, and Jim was sure his son wouldn't want to miss seeing the fighter.

Kevin couldn't see the jet from his seat, although when he heard Jim say that the fighter was there, Kevin immediately radioed the Iquitos tower. Although he was well beyond the normal fifty-mile contact distance and at the limits of his radio, Kevin was able to reach the tower on his third attempt. He reported his aircraft identification numbers, location, destination, and estimated time of arrival.

"Good morning. This is OB-1408. I'm at Pevas, en route from Islandia, at four thousand feet. What is the military doing here?" Kevin asked.[1]

The Iquitos tower reported poor reception of Kevin's transmission before repeating back his location and position. There was no comment to his question about the A-37 fighter jet. The tower asked, "When do you estimate landing on the Amazon River?"

Kevin responded, "I estimate landing in Iquitos in about forty minutes."

The Iquitos tower wanted to know if Kevin was on the water or in the air, and Kevin repeated his earlier radio message, "I'm in the air, at four thousand feet."

Iquitos tower confirmed, "You're at four thousand feet, off Pevas. OB-1408, call back in forty minutes at fifteen hundred feet . . ."

Kevin told Iquitos, "I'm eighty-seven miles out."

In the CIA's Citation jet, the two Americans told their Peruvian liaison, "He's talking to Iquitos." Meanwhile, the A-37 swooped beneath the Cessna and appeared briefly off to their left. By looking toward the back, Kevin could just make out, across the football-field-plus distance, the two dots of the air force pilots' helmets in the A-37 cockpit. But the plane soon disappeared from view, and Kevin returned his attention to flying.

Jim tried to watch the fighter jet, which had swooped back to his side of the Cessna, although still some distance behind the floatplane. As Jim turned in his seat to get another look back at the air force plane, he saw a puff of smoke come from the nose of the A-37.

He immediately told Kevin, "I just saw smoke from the front of the fighter." Jim wondered, *Are they shooting?* It was less than two minutes from the time Kevin contacted the control tower in Iquitos. But before Jim had a chance to verbalize his thought, the Cessna was engulfed in a cacophony of sound.

When Jim graduated from basic army training, he went to Florida to finalize his wedding plans with the Luttigs during the week between boot camp and his first army assignment with a helicopter unit in Colorado. Then he drove his Mustang to Colorado Springs and found an apartment where he would bring his bride after their marriage.

Roni decided to get married in Virginia since that's where she lived before going to college. Besides, Rose Parham and Grace Ferguson, her mother's former coworkers and cooks at Poquoson

Elementary School, had asked to do the reception. Another point in favor of a Virginia site was that it was closer to Terry and Wilma Bowers in Michigan, and closer to Dan Bowers and Jim and Roni's own friends still studying at Piedmont.

Jim and Roni's wedding took place on November 23, with all their family members and friends surrounding them. Everyone agreed that the couple, who were so alike in many ways yet complete opposites in others, were ideally suited to one another, even though they were young. Roni had just turned twenty that summer; Jim would be twenty-three in less than two months.

Uncle Sam had a few more surprises in store for Jim.

After one night each in Norfolk and downtown Denver, the newlyweds went to Breckenridge, Colorado, for the remainder of their honeymoon. Jim planned to spend four days at the resort, but the new Mrs. Bowers wanted to leave after only two days. Roni wanted to spend Thanksgiving in her new home, which, she pointed out to her husband, she hadn't even seen yet. She wanted to cook a big Thanksgiving dinner in their own place.

The disagreement ended when Jim said that Roni was right; it would be nice to spend Thanksgiving that way. They went back to Colorado Springs for a big chicken dinner with all the trimmings, including Roni's personal favorite, jellied cranberry sauce.

Within two weeks, Jim's duties as a helicopter mechanic sent him out "to the field," which meant more than a week without being able to contact Roni, who didn't really know anyone yet. Besides which, she had developed those annoying stomach problems again. This time, she ended up in the hospital with a diagnosis of appendicitis. Surgery to remove the inflamed organ ended that particular worry, and Jim even got a brief reprieve from the war games until after Roni's surgery.

Uncle Sam had a few more surprises in store for Jim. He was told at the end of his first year in Colorado that his final year in the army would have to be served in Germany—alone. If Jim wanted to take his wife, he would owe the army an extra two years overseas. Instead of paying the army the original two years which he had signed up for, Jim would owe the army a total of five years. As far as Jim and Roni were concerned, there was no question what they would do. They packed up, shipped their household goods, and embarked on a three-year adventure together.

Their time in Germany proved to be the making of Jim and Roni. The closeness they had forged during their first year of marriage in Colorado solidified even further in less familiar surroundings. They matured both personally and spiritually; they gained valuable experience, and they received ample confirmation that missionary service was definitely God's plan for their future.

Jim and Roni joined a Baptist church that worked primarily with military families in Wiesbaden. Although he hadn't finished his Bible school training, Jim had more Bible education than many of the men in the church and even was given the responsibilities of a deacon at his young age. He visited members of the congregation in their homes and invited their neighbors to attend, taught Sunday school, worked with the children's program, and discipled men who were new Christians.

Roni, like Jim, taught Sunday school and worked in AWANA, and sang in the church choir. She helped start a monthly program for the military wives, which included organizing Bible studies, craft get-togethers, outings to the surrounding countryside, and even trips to neighboring European countries.

But perhaps Roni's most lasting contribution to their church in Wiesbaden was helping start a Christian school where she taught for the remainder of her stay. She had a pastor's wife to help her with the two dozen students in kindergarten through eighth grades, designing bulletin boards, grading papers, and planning lessons that would make the children's learning experience fun.

The students of Independent Baptist Christian School caught Mrs. Bowers's enthusiastic commitment to follow God's leading in her life. Jennifer Kalnbach was only eight years old when Roni taught her. "I remember surrendering my life to missions . . . in Germany," Jennifer recalled. It was a commitment that would come to fruition in an unexpected manner.

But when she was still a little girl, Jennifer adored her teacher and AWANA leader, who accompanied the Kalnbach family on a trip to one of Germany's picturesque castles and ended up playing a ferocious card game with the family late into the night. "To say that Roni was competitive is an understatement," Jennifer remarked.

Debbie Walsh, one of the military wives who became a very close friend to Roni, was a teacher's aide at the Christian school. She noted that Roni's natural leadership and organizational skills were ideally suited to her growing responsibilities. Roni thrived in this new setting, making the most of her three years of elementary education and Bible training to teach her small class of students.

Debbie was serving as a parenting mentor to Roni, even though neither woman knew it at the time. Jim and Roni were like "a big brother and sister" to Doug and Debbie Walsh's three children. They attended Matt's softball games, and Roni taught both Amanda and Rachel. Jim and Roni baby-sat the Walsh children so their parents could get away by themselves, and the trio relished the adults' interest in their lives.

Roni shared with Debbie the disappointment she faced each month when she realized that she hadn't gotten pregnant

—again. When Doug and Debbie adopted a little girl from Bangladesh, Roni asked Debbie what it was like to be an adoptive parent. "How do you love a child that isn't your birth child? Does it bother you that she doesn't look like you?" Roni inquired.

Debbie told Roni that although she couldn't bear more children, she loved children so much and so wanted to have more in her home that she and her husband chose to adopt. "When I look at Hannah, I do not see color," Debbie explained. "I see my beautiful daughter." Roni would have reason to remember Debbie's words one day.

While Roni taught school, Jim spent roughly eight hours a day repairing combat helicopters. He enjoyed a ten-minute bike ride to work, mostly through cherry orchards on back roads. His duties weren't demanding; often there were no helicopters in need of repair, so he and another mechanic would be sent to other U.S. military bases to do repairs. Most times he'd be home by the end of the day. In many ways, it was similar to any civilian job.

The Bowers and Luttig families back in the States kept in touch with Jim and Roni by phone and letter. Dan, Jim's younger brother, once sent a care package. "Exactly the same stuff they could get on base," as Dan recalls. But the college student only had his own experience in Brazil to go by, so he sent macaroni and cheese, hot chocolate and drink mixes, and other foods that Americans welcomed in South America.

By this time, Jim's older brother, Phil, had a job with Continental Airlines. For Terry and Wilma's twenty-fifth wedding anniversary, Phil gave them tickets to Germany. Jim and Roni took two weeks to tour Europe with Jim's parents. They saw the sights of London, Paris, Berlin, and Amsterdam, and drove through Belgium, Switzerland, and Austria on a tremendous vacation.

During their stay in Germany, Jim had thirty days off each year, and Roni had three-and-a-half months' vacation each summer. They also took advantage of many four-day weekends to see a lot of the world. They flew standby on military transports and sometimes spent the night in airports while waiting for a connection. They typically carried backpacks and stayed in bed-and-breakfasts, which proved to be the best way to meet and enjoy the people around them. Visiting so many countries was an unexpected bonus of their extended military tour, a veritable gift from God.

One of Roni's growing concerns was her inability to get pregnant. She thought that perhaps the constant activity, combined with the stresses from trying to run a school, might be taking their toll physically. Maybe once she was able to relax completely, nature would take its course. She confided to a few close friends that she worried a bit but added, "God knows the perfect time."

Most people would never have known that Roni had a care in the world. During her fierce battles at the pinochle table or other games, she became something of a legend among her friends for her take-no-prisoners attitude.

When Jim and Roni left Germany they told the church in Wiesbaden, "We're going to be missionaries in Brazil." The church sent out the young couple as their missionaries to the Amazon, beginning to mail monthly checks as if they were already on the mission field.

Wilma and Terry had returned to the States from Belo Horizonte, Brazil, in 1989 as Terry's health showed signs of marked deterioration. Tests revealed that he had cancer. After their three-week anniversary trip with Jim and Roni in Europe, the Bowers parents reached North Carolina and literally collapsed. At Jim's discharge from the army just a few months later, Terry wasn't well enough to go. Instead, Dan and Wilma kept Roni company (and rescued her from the seedy motel where she and Jim had been billeted) while Jim finished mustering out.

That very afternoon, over a foot-long sub, Roni said, "We'll rest for a little, but we need to get back to school and finish up." As usual, she was eager to move on to the next thing looming on the horizon—in this case, completing the final year of college so she and Jim could become missionaries. The plan was for Jim to finish aviation training and Roni to get her degree in elementary education.

In February of 1990, once they were no longer at the beck and call of the United States Army, Jim and Roni looked for jobs. They found a little apartment and started saving money for the fall semester at Piedmont. Although Jim was working for an airlines subcontractor, he still wasn't making enough to pay the high fees of flight instruction. It soon became obvious that there wasn't going to be any miracle money scheme for Jim to be able to afford his flight training.

Jim broke the news to his dad, "I'm not going to be a missionary pilot." It was hard to say since that had been Jim's unspoken goal for as long as he could remember, and he expected someday to take his dad's place in Brazil. Instead of suffering terrible disappointment, however, Terry expressed enormous relief to his wife. "It's so dangerous now with the drug traffic down there," he told Wilma. Terry himself hadn't been flying along the Amazon since 1987; it wasn't something he wanted for his son.

Terry Bowers had taught aviation mechanics courses at Piedmont until his cancer progressed so rapidly that he was unable to continue. Jim took over for his dad in the spring of 1991. That helped with Jim and Roni's tuition costs, since Jim now was officially a staff member. Their load was more hectic than ever; Jim still worked full-time, taught part-time, and took classes part-time. He often visited his dad at the hospital where Terry underwent a series of surgeries. Roni, too, worked while taking classes.

Despite their heavy work and school loads, Jim and Roni both sang in the church choir, taught Sunday school, and worked in junior church. Jim discipled other men and became the AWANA commander, directed the church's program for visiting members and newcomers, and served as a deacon. Roni took part in the women's group organized specifically to pray for and encourage missionaries and raise money for special missionary projects. All of this was excellent training for missionary work.

Looking back later, Jim would wonder how they juggled such nightmarish schedules. Even at the time, the couple deplored the lack of time they were able to spend together. "Having a daily time of Bible reading and prayer is almost impossible," Roni wrote. "Jim and I hardly ever see each other because of our work schedules, so it's even harder for us to have devotions together."

The career missionaries remembered Jim and Roni entering into their summer missions program with enthusiasm.

Jim and Roni knew that missionary aviation wasn't in their future because of the impossibility of finances, but they were quite certain that missions of some sort definitely was. They weren't sure where they would end up, but God's direction still seemed to say, "Missions."

Terry died in July of 1991, shattering the Bowers family circle. Life continued to barrel along for Jim and Roni, but after almost seven years of marriage, the couple still showed no signs of having children. Again Roni attributed the cause to incredibly high levels of stress: the death of Jim's father; trying to finish school while working full-time; and fulfilling responsibilities in their local church. No wonder they hadn't had children! At least that was probably the reason. But there was always a question at the back of Roni's mind.

In 1992, a full year before they would finally graduate from Piedmont, Jim and Roni contacted ABWE to see about taking a trip to South America. Since Jim wasn't going to be a missionary pilot after all, he wondered where the mission board under which his parents had served could use a couple with the skills he and Roni possessed. His heart was definitely in South America, specifically, the Amazon region.

That's when Don Trott, ABWE's enlistment director, suggested the Bowers look at Peru. ABWE missionaries Andy and Diane Large, who had grown up as MKs in Peru, owned a houseboat that they operated out of Iquitos, the key city of Peru's Amazon region. The Larges also owned a house on the outskirts of Iquitos near the port where they docked their boat. They lived on the river for several weeks at a time, preaching and teaching in villages along a 250-mile stretch of the Amazon and its tributaries. They had been doing this for a decade and could certainly use help. Maybe that type of work would interest Jim and Roni Bowers.

In the six weeks they spent looking over the work in Peru, Jim and Roni got a good feel for the work ABWE missionaries were attempting along the Amazon. The Larges and Chuck and Carrie Porter, who'd been working along the river since 1960, had a well-organized system of evangelizing. They divided the Amazon River into two 250-mile stretches so that, between the two couples, they could train national leaders in the existing churches and help form new churches all along the river.

Andy had started a Bible institute in Caballacocha where pastors and lay leaders from towns within a 50-mile radius came periodically for a week of intensive training. The national leaders could take that information back to their towns and villages and share it with leaders who hadn't been able to attend. The Peruvians were then better equipped to lead programs and pastor churches. The small monetary investment paid big dividends in the lives of Peruvian people.

The career missionaries remembered Jim and Roni entering into their summer missions program with enthusiasm. "One thing that impressed us when they were in the village, they visited every house on their own, not with the missionaries," Carrie Porter said.

Andy Large was grateful that Jim helped out, even though he didn't speak the language and wasn't completely familiar with all his surroundings. "I did something with Jim that I've never done with any other [short-term missionary]," Andy said. "When one of the pastors died from a snakebite and I had to preach that night, I asked Jim if he would take the body and the family back to their town. He was willing to do it, even though he spent the whole day doing that."

Jim remembers trying to figure out where he was going, asking the widow at frequent intervals, "Is this it?" Little did he realize that one day he would be as familiar with the Amazon and its tributaries as he was with the streets of his hometown in Michigan.

It was after a children's meeting in a town called Huanta where Roni taught (Jim translated) and several children prayed to receive Christ as Savior, that she said to Jim, "I think this is the place where God wants us to be missionaries." Her statement reaffirmed Jim's own conviction. Jim and Roni returned to the States confident of their future in the Amazon region of Peru and more determined than ever to get on with their life's work.

After Terry's death in 1991, Wilma had given in to Jim and Roni's urging that she live near them. Terry had said just before he died that he wanted her to get a job at Piedmont Bible College. "I think you'd make a good receptionist," Terry told his wife.

Within hours of Terry's death, Wilma had a phone call offering her a job as a receptionist at Piedmont. She would take the place of a woman who had suddenly quit after more than twenty years at the post. Wilma looked on it as God's seal of approval. She accepted the job and lived in a town house not far from Jim and Roni's mobile home.

As students passed her in the halls, Wilma often prayed, *Lord, let one of these students take Terry's and my place on the Amazon.* She prepared a letter sharing that prayer request with the churches and individuals who had supported her and her husband for so many years. Jim took the letter home to type on his word processor and duplicate.

The following day, Jim entered Wilma's office, crouched down next to her desk, and said, "Mom, Roni and I will be the ones. We're going to fill that gap."

Wilma's first thought was, *Oh, dear God, Roni will be the one that makes this ministry go.* Wilma knew from experience that it is often missionary wives who determine whether or not their husbands can stick it out. Home becomes even more of a shelter for the family overseas than it is in North America. Wilma could see that Roni was ideally suited to the task.

When Jim and Roni graduated from Piedmont in May of 1993, he had a degree in Bible; Roni received degrees in both elementary education and Bible. They had challenged each other to excel in their work (Roni graduated with honors), had carried incredible loads at work and in their church, and had faced severe emotional trauma with the death of Jim's father. They were ready to begin pursuit of a missionary career, their long-awaited goal.

CHAPTER SIX

. . . And if God should choose
and my life I lose . . .

10:47 A.M., APRIL 20, 2001

Jim knew instantly what was happening, thanks to that split second of wondering about the puff of smoke. As soon as he heard the noise and felt the jolting and battering of the floatplane, he knew the fighter jet was shooting at them. The barrage of bullets pierced through the Cessna's metal frame in a storm of smoke and heat.

Kevin grabbed his radio and yelled to the Iquitos tower, "They're killing us! They're killing us!"[1]

And that certainly seemed to be the intent. Jim saw a huge crack in the windshield in front of his head where a bullet had exited. But he didn't pay much attention to it just then, because part of the mass confusion in those first few moments was the thick smoke that filled the little cabin. A fire flared up like a blowtorch through the floor of the Cessna under Kevin's seat at Roni's feet.

Jim called to Kevin, "Where's the fire extinguisher?" Kevin pointed to the container on the door next to his left knee, never taking his eyes from the controls where he switched off the engine and fuel as he sent the Cessna into a dive through the clouds toward the trees. If he could keep the plane aloft long enough, Kevin knew he might make it to the Amazon River, which eventually curved back around after making a huge arc around the rain forest below.

"Iquitos, this is 1408!," he yelled again to the tower nearly one hundred miles away. "Do you copy me? Do you copy me?"[2] For the next ninety seconds, Kevin continued attempting to elicit a response from Iquitos while diving toward the river but heard nothing.

Jim's moment of panic when the little handheld fire extinguisher refused to function subsided slightly when he realized he hadn't pulled the pin that freed the mechanism. He leaned over the back of his seat, aiming the extinguisher on the fire that billowed from the floor and reignited as fast as he put it out.

"Open the windows!" Kevin instructed Jim. Jim swiveled around to the front long enough to create the ventilation that would permit visibility in the cabin. He briefly registered the fact that Roni was slumped over and that she never moved her legs from the flames that burst through the Cessna's floor. Charity lay on the floor at Cory's feet, one side of her face covered with blood. Jim placed her back on Roni's lap, unable to comprehend what all that blood might mean. He was completely preoccupied with the fire. If he couldn't keep that from spreading to the fuel tanks, they would all explode in a fiery ball over the treetops.

"We've got to get out of here!" Cory shouted several times. The choking, blinding smoke and intense heat would have frightened any adult, let alone a young child. Jim held Cory's head to the window with his left hand, and continued fighting the blazing fire with the fire extinguisher in his right hand.

Spray, spray, spray. Pause to see the fire go out then it *whoosh* back in again. Spray some more. Jim's attention narrowed to that spot on the floor where the fire blazed through, although he swung around once, long enough to notice that Kevin had been able to get the plane back over water and was about to touch down. *Thank God!* Jim thought. *We're going to make it!*

When Kevin went to step on the rudder and straighten out the Cessna, his right foot refused to function. Knowing he'd been hit but unaware of the extent of his injuries, Kevin feared that landing heavily to one side would cause the plane to flip over; however, there was nothing else he could do.

10:50 A.M., APRIL 20, 2001

The Cessna smacked down on the Amazon River, sending torrents of water over the broken windshield and into the cabin. The floatplane swung around sharply, throwing all the occupants to one side. Jim thought, *It's over. We're going to cartwheel and that's it.* He expected oblivion at any moment. Instead, the plane came to an abrupt stop, an eerie silence following the chaotic hail of bullets, fire, and smoke that accompanied the one-and-a-half minute plummet from four thousand feet.

Although Kevin had taken immediate preventive measures to eliminate the awful possibility of explosion, a fuel line had ignited before he'd been able to complete his action. Fire filled the cabin, and Jim still feared an imminent explosion. He told Cory to jump out of the plane.

Cory looked down into fire-covered water where spilled fuel blazed on the surface of the river. He hesitated to plunge into that mess, but his father urged him on. "Jump, Cory! Jump!" Jim insisted. So Cory jumped—fully clothed and still wearing his tennis shoes—into the middle of the fire on the river. Jim saw Cory struggling and thought about his shoes. "Take your shoes off!" Jim yelled.

Kevin went to exit through the door beside him and discovered the extent of the damage to his legs only when he fell out the door and onto a float. He reached back into the plane for his life jacket but found it had been rendered useless by bullet holes. Kevin flopped into the river, swimming away from the burning Cessna.

Jim was ready to jump out of the floatplane himself when he remembered that Roni and Charity were helpless. He turned back and wrestled Roni out of her seat belt, dragging her and Charity out of the plane with him. Although the flames that surrounded them were intense, he escaped with nothing more than singed hair.

Once he jumped into the water, Jim, too, swam away from the aircraft, pushing away the blazing fuel with surprising ease. Cradling Roni in the crook of his left arm, with Charity nestled between them, Jim began treading water.

Six weeks after graduating from Piedmont Bible College, Jim and Roni arrived at ABWE's candidate class on the campus of Baptist Bible College in Clarks Summit, Pennsylvania. They were attending the intensive training and information seminar ABWE conducted for individuals who hoped to join the mission.

During this period, mission officials explained in great detail ABWE's policies on raising financial support. New missionaries needed to contact churches and individuals who would pledge monthly sums. That money would be sent to ABWE, earmarked for the specific missionaries. At mission headquarters, staff members recorded the donations and sent receipts to each donor, keeping records for the IRS. Missionaries, too, had to keep meticulous records. Anytime they asked to be reimbursed from their account at the mission headquarters, they had to supply receipts and expense reports that tallied.

Missionaries from the more than forty-five countries where ABWE operated told about the places where they worked and the different kinds of evangelistic outreach programs, ranging from orphanages and hospitals to centers for the physically disabled and schools. It was a time for prospective missionaries to learn where and how they might work, a time for intense self-examination and soul-searching: *Is this truly what God wants for me?*

Jim and Roni already knew they were headed for Peru. Candidate classes didn't change anything, but they learned more about the practical aspects of missions, such as reporting to ABWE's headquarters and how they would function as members of the missionary team, called a "field council" in most countries. They learned about the mission's policy of not funding national works but encouraging nationals themselves to support their own efforts at whatever level they could afford. They also met the man who was just taking over as executive administrator of South America, David Southwell.

Jim knew that
he wanted to build a boat.

Dave had been a missionary with ABWE first in Brazil and then in Portugal. He was familiar with the Bowers family name, although the Southwells hadn't worked in the same region of Brazil as Terry and Wilma. Dave's wife, Evelyn, had been born in Brazil and lived there for most of her childhood. Her parents, too, had been missionaries with ABWE.

Dave didn't know Jim and Roni personally until he became their administrator, but he grew to love them. He recognized in their straightforward, hardworking approach to life the qualities that make missions—or any other endeavor—a success. "I don't care how many Bill Gates-dot.com type of people we have in the world," he said. ". . . ABWE only exists because of people like Jim and Roni Bowers."

Immediately upon their official acceptance by ABWE, Jim and Roni made another trip to Peru for a few weeks to gather additional facts. Jim knew that he wanted to build a boat. Unlike the missionaries already in Peru, however, he and Roni would live on their boat full-time. They'd stay on the river and make occasional trips back to Iquitos. That way, they wouldn't have to set up two houses or have to maintain two properties.

Jim and Roni looked at the missionaries' boats, talked to Peruvian boatbuilders, and found out the pros and cons of the various designs in existence. They asked endless questions and formulated plans.

Then they moved back to Muskegon, Michigan, where Wilma now lived while caring for Jim's ailing grandmother. Jim met with Dr. Bill Rudd, Calvary Church's senior pastor, to ask if Calvary would take on some of the couple's financial support. Bill Rudd firmly believed—and still does—that a pastor shouldn't just load a church's missions roster with his own cronies. In the event that a pastor moves on, the church is still responsible to support the missionaries under its financial umbrella.

Bill Rudd told Jim that the church would have to vote on whether or not to sponsor them. Not that the pastor had any doubt Jim and Roni would be welcomed with open arms.

"You so quickly [grasp] the authenticity of their character and relationship with God and their passion for serving Him," Bill Rudd stated. "They are very relational people, very giving of themselves. Within days of arriving in town, they'd be asking, 'What can we do? Where do you need us?' "

The behind-the-scenes work to which Jim and Roni seemed to gravitate impressed the missions-minded church and its pastoral staff. The unique nature of their intended ministry in Peru—living on a houseboat on the Amazon River—piqued people's interest. And Jim and Roni's obvious dedication about the task facing them earned them enthusiastic support, both financial and emotional.

The couple joined a Sunday school class of mostly older couples, partly because Roni found it extremely difficult to be around young couples whose conversation revolved around their children. Testing revealed that Jim and Roni couldn't have children of their own. While Roni had accepted this difficult reality as part of God's plan, it didn't mean that she wanted to pour salt in an open wound.

Bill and Pat Rexford were one of the couples in the Sunday school class Jim and Roni wiggled their way into. At first Pat thought, *Surely the missionaries-in-training have made a mistake. They must have meant to join a class of younger people.* Pat remembers them asking, "When are you going to have us over for dinner?" She just couldn't imagine that a couple barely into their thirties could be interested in hanging around "a bunch of old fogeys like us." But Jim and Roni made it clear that they weren't especially concerned about the age difference. They joined in the hayrides, bonfires, and other social activities in addition to the regular Sunday classes.

A member of Calvary's missions committee, Wilma Bowers was thrilled to see her home church taking such an interest in her son and daughter-in-law. She introduced Jim to pastors of other churches in Michigan that had supported her and Terry during their thirty-year missionary career. Many of those churches pledged part of the monthly finances Jim and Roni would need to live in Peru.

At one church they received more than finances. When it was obvious that Jim and Roni wouldn't be able to have children but that Roni was so desperate to be a mother, Wilma casually mentioned to Jim that one of the churches where they would speak was within a half hour of the Baptist Children's Home in Mt. Pleasant, Michigan. The agency placed the children of unwed mothers—mostly teenagers—with Christian families.

Although the waiting period could be long and there were no guarantees, Wilma thought her son and his wife might like to look into the home and see if they qualified to be adoptive parents. Wilma was careful to mention this only to Jim, reading between the lines that adoption might be an option. She didn't want to risk offending her daughter-in-law by discussing it openly.

At a church where she was speaking to the women's group, Roni, in an unprecedented move for someone who kept her thoughts to herself, succumbed to a strong urge to tell the group that she and Jim were considering adoption.

"I can't believe I'm saying this," she admitted to the women, "but for some reason, God wants me to share with you what we're thinking." Roni didn't go into specifics about where they might adopt but talked of the infertility struggles she had faced over the past decade and her heart's desire to raise a child.

What Roni didn't realize was that the director of the Baptist Children's Home was sitting in the audience. When she and Jim reached the home the following day, the director immediately recognized her speaker from the previous night. What Jim and Roni learned encouraged them, and they decided that this route might be the means of raising a family after all.

Pam Hewitt, a member of Calvary Church and an MK from Peru—she had grown up in the Amazon region where her parents, Chuck and Carrie Porter, worked—bonded with Roni almost from the instant the Bowers couple arrived at the church in Muskegon. While Roni was speaking about the work she and Jim planned to do in Peru, Pam was, by her own admission, "homesick and missing Peru. . . . To think that Jim and Roni were going, I was a little bit emotional about their opportunity to minister to the people that I love."

As she was talking, Roni started to cry because her heart was so burdened for the people of Peru. The two women noticed each other's tears and struck up a deep friendship. Roni asked Pam to pray about her childlessness. Pam would say years later, "I felt greatly honored because I could tell that it was something very close to her heart. . . . What drew us even closer together was praying for God's will in their life."

The friendship was one of mutual accountability and strengthening. Roni shared her frustration with Pam about individuals who behaved in ways she thought were wrong. She struggled with her anger at them. "I don't want to feel this way; I know it isn't right," Roni would say. She and Pam prayed together as Roni consciously worked on adjusting her own attitude.

Pam explained, "Roni consciously focused her mind on the good in life, even though she had a constant ache inside of her when she was waiting for God's answer in the way of children. It was a constant ache, I know. . . . She just looked on what good there was to see. That is something that always impressed me about her. She really made a habit of building people up."

Jim and Roni finally connected with Bill and Pat Rexford's grown children who attended Calvary Church. They met Todd and MaryBeth Rexford at a home meeting one evening when they were talking about their prospective work in Peru. After the meeting, Roni went to the kitchen to help clean up and started talking with MaryBeth. Roni learned that MaryBeth had gone through two miscarriages after the birth of a son. The two women forged a friendship over their common heartache of infertility. The bond lasted even after MaryBeth eventually bore two more children.

Todd Rexford and Jim Bowers, too, became good friends. The two couples often socialized with Todd's parents on the senior Rexfords' fifteen-acre property outside town. Jim and Roni also got acquainted with Todd's sister and brother-in-law, Paula and Jim Kramer, and with other thirty-something couples at Calvary Church.

It was difficult for Roni, seeing all those squealing children when her own arms ached with emptiness, but she was determined to accept whatever God allowed in her life without complaining. The margins of her Bible and her journals were filled with prayers begging God for a child, but filling out the papers at the Baptist Children's Home was the extent of Roni's public discourse on this painful topic.

It was at Todd and MaryBeth Rexfords' house that Jim and Roni sketched out the preliminary design for their houseboat. MaryBeth phoned Bill and Gloria Rudd, telling the pastor and his wife, "You need to come and see something important."

The Rudds hurried over to find a boat sketched out to scale in chalk—on Todd and MaryBeth's driveway. MaryBeth got a toilet tank lid and placed it in the boat's bathroom; pots and pans stood in the spot where Jim and Roni's stove would be positioned. Those early plans were refined and formally drawn by an architect, but it was typical of Jim and Roni to involve other people in the initial stages.

On December 19, 1994,
Cory James Bowers became theirs.

The financial support for Jim and Roni was coming in quickly. The church in Wiesbaden, Germany, started sending monthly checks from the time Jim and Roni left Germany to finish school. Churches around Michigan, as well as the church Roni's parents attended in Panama City, Florida, pledged support. With the addition of several more churches in North Carolina, Jim and Roni reached their financial requirements within the year.

Less than six months before leaving the United States for intensive Spanish language study in Costa Rica, the Bowers received an incredible gift. The phone call that started their euphoria came one November day when Jim and Roni were staying with Wilma.

Wilma told Jim and Roni that someone from the Baptist Children's Home was on the line to talk to them—either of them. Subsequent squealing let Wilma know something was happening. Roni bounded down the stairs two at a time to exclaim, "We have a baby!"

A baby boy, born early in November, was only ten days old when Jim and Roni found out that a teenaged mother and father chose the Bowers couple to be the parents of their child.

Jim and Roni had waited and prayed for years for this moment to arrive. The six-week-long waiting period during which the birth parents could change their mind seemed interminable. On December 19, 1994, Cory James Bowers became theirs.

Friends still talk about the pride that gleamed on Jim and Roni's faces as they showed off baby Cory to everyone who would stand still long enough to take a peek. The healthy, sturdy little boy was a delight to the parents who had waited with love in their hearts for a child on whom to lavish their affection.

But just because they were besotted didn't mean that they were pushovers. Roni had been raised under strict discipline, and even though this was her first child, she naturally eased into the role she had seen modeled all her life.

Cory was trained that bedtime was for sleeping. Roni read him stories and prayed with him—even though he was only a couple of months old—then said, "It's time to go to sleep now." She steeled herself to ignore any whimpering or crying and insisted that her mother do likewise. "He has to learn," she told Gloria. After all, Roni had completely checked him over from head to toe and knew full well that he didn't need anything to eat, wore a dry diaper, and didn't have a rash or sore anywhere on his body.

Roni kept herself on a strict schedule, the ideal environment in which to raise a baby. She needed a good eight hours of sleep each night, so she went to bed shortly after Cory. While he napped, she did ironing or other household chores. She had almost four months in which to establish a routine before leaving for language study in Costa Rica.

For Jim, who spoke fluent Portuguese, Spanish came fairly easy. He skipped the first trimester. For Roni, who spoke only English, language acquisition was a struggle. Not only did she have the care of an infant, she and Jim realized before they left the States that they would only learn Spanish fluently if they lived with a Spanish-speaking family while studying. So when they arrived in Costa Rica, they moved in with a family that spoke no English at all. It was difficult to communicate but provided the perfect incentive to learn quickly.

An added frustration for Roni was that, in the Latin culture, she had little value. Jim as head of the family was certainly important, and Cory as a child and the family heir, no less, certainly rated. But as a woman, Roni was regarded as nothing more important than a piece of furniture. She really disliked being overlooked, disliked the fact that Daisy, their Costa Rican hostess, did all the things she was used to doing for Jim and Cory, and disliked not being acknowledged in that culture.

Applying the same competitiveness to learning Spanish that she had to her college classes, Roni set herself a strenuous program, even though—or perhaps because—she couldn't keep attending the full schedule of daily classes. Once Jim got home from school, Roni went to places she had established for practicing what she had learned with a tutor. She was far more disciplined in that respect than Jim. Because of his fluency in Portuguese, Jim was able to communicate sooner than Roni, but his grammar and vocabulary were sometimes sloppy.

Within a matter of months, Jim preached several times and Roni taught women—all in Spanish. The immersion paid off in several respects. They learned the language out of necessity and kept using it day after day, always bearing in mind that it was essential to be able to converse upon arrival in Peru. Having visited three times and not being able to speak the language showed them how imperative it was that they reach Peru being able to talk to people. They also got over some of the cultural adjustments of living in a developing country before adding the ministry dimension on top of that.

Their nine months of language study was shorter than most people's, but Jim and Roni were determined if nothing else. They were impatient to get to their work in Peru, the goal that had been out in front of them for so many years, and which they were now so close to achieving.

During those months in Costa Rica, Jim had gotten e-mail

—something rare among missionaries in those days—to order construction supplies, which he then had delivered to Bill and Pat Rexford's barn in Muskegon. Jim's plan was to gather a work team who could prefabricate sections of the houseboat and ship them to Peru to be assembled on-site.

He made numerous phone calls and spent thousands of dollars on the materials, aided by friends in Muskegon. Pastor and Mrs. Rudd had a friend in Elkhart, Indiana, who ran a recreational vehicle business. The Rudds recognized from the preliminary chalk sketches that Jim and Roni's boat would be along the lines of an RV and put Jim in touch with Bill and Carol Stankovich. The Stankoviches in turn contacted friends who built the prefabrication house structure without charging for labor. Jim Kramer and his brother-in-law made use of their connections in the metalworking business to acquire large quantities of aluminum for the boat hull at manufacturer's cost. Don Hankin provided input into the early design and also produced preliminary drawings of the hull.

Once again, Jim and Roni were involving their support team personally in their work. People didn't just give money toward the boat; they helped gather supplies or purchased a specific part or piece of equipment. One member of the church paid for an engine; someone else bought the steering wheel; another bought aluminum sheets. They could look at the finished product one day and say, "That's my window." Or, "I paid for that wall." It gave them a sense of ownership in Jim and Roni's work.

Chapter Seven

. . . Though my foe may slay me,
I will serve the Lord. . . .

11:00 A.M., APRIL 20, 2001

The survivors expected the Cessna to explode. Their first thought was to get as far from the wreck as possible to avoid injury from fire and flying debris. It was Kevin who first realized that the plane, listing heavily and sinking fast in the water, would eventually flip over and remain buoyant, thanks to the air-filled chambers in the floats.

The trio watched from about fifty yards away as the aircraft turned over in the water, extinguishing the fire. Kevin called to Jim to swim back to the plane.

"We can hang on to the floats," he suggested, "and safely wait for rescue there."

Jim asked, "Why not swim to shore? I can keep treading water." He didn't expect the plane to continue floating and figured they could keep on as they were indefinitely, certainly long enough to reach the riverbank.

Kevin told Jim, "I can't swim. My legs were shot up pretty bad."

They headed immediately for the floats. Kevin climbed on one, Cory on the other, with Jim at the end of one float, holding on to Roni and Charity. That's when the full significance of Roni and Charity's death finally penetrated the initial chaos, adding unimaginable tragedy to the unthinkable horror this day had become.

Jim told Cory, "You know Mom and Charity didn't make it, don't you? They're in heaven with Jesus now."

Cory said he knew. He would say much later that he, too, had seen Charity's face covered in blood. The bullet that lodged in the back of Charity's head had first penetrated Roni's heart, leaving only holes in the back and front of her shirt to mark the ammunition's path. Mother and daughter were killed by a single bullet.

The Peruvian air force's A-37 circled repeatedly at treetop height over the crash site, while the CIA's surveillance Citation jet circled from a greater distance. Not knowing if the strafing would continue or how they would be rescued, the survivors literally cried out to God as they huddled around the sinking wreckage of the Cessna.

11:05 A.M., APRIL 20, 2001

Kevin made his socks and belt serve double duty as tourniquets for his badly injured leg. Although the flesh wound on his left calf gaped, it was his right leg that was the main concern. A profusely bleeding calf and shattered bones meant that little more than skin attached Kevin's foot to his leg. Despite the makeshift tourniquets, Kevin's leg continued to bleed as precious minutes ticked by. Since they were out in the river's swiftly moving current, they figured there was less danger from piranha attacks. But the loss of blood was more than enough danger of its own.

The survivors floated downstream for a half hour when they spotted a canoe in the distance. They called, whistled, and waved, hoping to attract the local people's notice and—they hoped—be rescued by them. They soon realized that their gesturing and calling were superfluous; this was their rescue party. The canoe headed straight for them, never wavering. It was actually two canoes, one large canoe and a much smaller one.

Cory was loaded into the smaller boat, which headed straight for shore. The others were pulled into the larger canoe, which drifted toward the town's main port. Jim and Kevin repeatedly requested to be taken to a more private landing spot—anywhere not in the path of the double-decker commercial passenger boat that would arrive in port at any minute.

Kevin's leg continued to spill blood. It pooled in the bottom of the large dugout. Jim's belt offered a more substantial tourniquet, and a canoe paddle under Kevin's leg helped stabilize the mangled leg, but his medical condition was still grave. The Peruvians recognized the serious threat to Kevin's survival if the bleeding could not be stopped.

11:15 A.M., APRIL 20, 2001

The rescue party had come from Huanta, a town of about six hundred people where Jim and Roni Bowers preached and taught in their missionary work on the Amazon River. Although local residents had ringside seats of the entire incident, they were afraid to venture out too quickly in case the firing continued. Once they realized the shooting had stopped with the downing of the Cessna, they hopped into canoes to pick up any survivors, reaching the missionaries about a half hour after the shoot down occurred.

The Peruvians were astonished to see the familiar faces of their missionary friends. When the large canoe drifted up to Huanta's port, wailing and shrieking greeted the passengers. Word quickly spread that Monica (the Spanish name by which Roni had been known) and her baby daughter were dead. Friends of the Bowers family and curious townspeople quickly converged on the scene to find out for themselves if this terrible news was true. Pastor Ernesto Flores rushed down to the port—not even bothering to put on a shirt—where he learned the horrible news. He couldn't believe his ears weren't playing tricks on him.

Jim was given a bar of soap to wash off jet fuel that stung his arms and chest. He scrubbed vigorously with the soap to relieve the burning pain while trying to shield the bodies of his wife and daughter from curious eyes. He moved Charity out of the way of those tending to Kevin's leg, placing the baby girl on top of his wife. He asked for a large sheet of plastic to cover the bodies. The black plastic drape protected them from the inquisitive gaze of the gathering crowd.

Jim's more immediate worry, however, was Cory's whereabouts.

Jim, Roni, and Cory Bowers arrived in Peru on March 1, 1996, to join the group of ABWE missionaries in Iquitos. Evangelization along the river had been going on for more than three decades. ABWE missionaries had started and were still helping to run a Bible institute and a deaf school and had started numerous churches in Iquitos and in river towns. Jim and Roni would be part of the river outreach.

Their first year was to be spent in orientation, honing their Spanish-speaking abilities and becoming acquainted with eleven Baptist churches in Iquitos and thirteen more on the river.

Jim and Roni lived in Andy and Di Large's house while the Larges were on furlough. The house, about a mile from the Iquitos port, was an ideal location from which Jim and Roni could make short trips on the river in their own speedboat, once it arrived in their shipment of goods from the United States.

Within the same gated property across the cement courtyard, Pastor Javier and Karina Manihuari lived with their four children. "At first, Roni didn't seem like a person we would be able to be close to, but that was before she got used to the place, settled in, and became accustomed to where she was living," Pastor Javier recounted.

"Our friendship began because they liked to take part in volleyball games and things. They joked with us. Roni and Jim would come over and walk right into the kitchen. They'd say, 'What's in the pot?' They made us feel like they trusted us to be their friends. We didn't have to knock; we could go right into their house."

Pastor Javier appreciated Jim and Roni volunteering to help, asking, "What can we do?" Jim and Roni jointly ran youth group meetings on Saturday nights. They devised events for the young people at church that would also attract young people from outside the church. The contests they developed had a spiritual side as well as a fun side—Scripture memory and church attendance, combined with sporting events—and the prizes included dinner out and a river trip. Jim and Roni succeeded in getting youth participation in the local church.

"They had more specials from the young people than we could accommodate in one service," Pastor Javier said.

In preparation for the day when they would work out on the river, Jim spoke many times in nearly all the Iquitos churches, sometimes making mistakes that set the congregation to laughing. He would say, "OK, teach me the right way to say it." And then he'd start over and say it correctly. That willingness to be taught impressed the Peruvians.

Never forgetting that her first priority was to her husband and young son, Roni organized her schedule in order to be involved in individual outreach to Peruvians. She taught women's Bible studies and children's Sunday school classes.

Karina Manihuari, her neighbor and a local pastor's wife, was encouraged by Roni when the ladies' group hit a slump. "Don't quit, Karina; keep going," Roni encouraged her friend. "Whatever you need, I'll help you with it." Roni was true to her word, not just taking turns teaching, but organizing events for the ladies.

At another Iquitos church, Teodora Sifuentes recalled a time when Roni was asked to speak on the spur of the moment. Roni readily consented, talking about her struggles with infertility. "The ladies listened because she was sharing from her own life. They knew that she cared about them," Teodora said.

Peruvians felt welcome at the Bowerses' home. Their courtyard often served as the location for intense volleyball matches, preceded or followed by explanations of the gospel message. Tracts that were handed out to opponents were explained during breaks or after the games. Jim and Roni were letting the Peruvian people get close to them, preaching with their lives as well as their mouths.

Pastor Javier paid attention to Jim's attitude to the Peruvians. "He could be very, very busy, but he would always take time for people. He preached that you should love your neighbor as yourself. They also lived it. This place was like a park. Everybody that wanted to could come in when Jim and Roni were here. When anyone came in, they greeted them, hugging and kissing them. The people said, 'We need to listen to what they say because they are treating us so well.' "

During that year of introduction, Jim continued to make progress on the houseboat. Before going to Peru, he spent countless hours at Bill and Pat Rexfords' barn as friends helped assemble portions of the boat. He gathered the remaining materials to be shipped to Peru. He would send everything in two containers the size of a tractor-trailer without the wheels.

But getting the items into Peru without having to pay arbitrarily assigned import fees—known to amount to well above the value of the goods themselves—was a real concern. Jim spent hours working with an attorney in Lima to get exoneration from the fees, something akin to tax exemption. Jim and Roni weren't importing their goods for sale but for use in their mission work. Jim knew that the legal headache would be worthwhile once his request was granted, and it would prove helpful to other missionaries when they imported their goods.

When he finally had the exoneration in hand, Jim shipped all their goods from the States. He was able to clear them through customs in Peru within a few months and without having to pay

Roni Luttig as a toddler.

Jim in Brazil, 1966.

Roni and Jim at Piedmont Bible College.

The Bowers family expands: John and Gloria Luttig, Roni, Jim, Wilma and Terry Bowers—November 23, 1985.

Jim and Roni traveled throughout Europe—East Berlin, 1988.

Roni and ten-months-old Cory, in Costa Rica, 1995.

The houseboat under construction, 1997.

Leaders of churches along the Ampiyacu River review ministry materials—Purqaurquillo, 1997.

Offering counsel to church leaders was a major part of Jim's ministry, 1998.

Iquitos 1999.

Cory with friends in Caballo Cocha, 1999.

Grandma Bowers travelled on board for six weeks—Orellana, 2000.

Some of the believers from the church in Huanta—June 1999.

Alejandro, one of the leaders of the church in Purcaurquillo, and his family with their new two-day-old baby—June 1999.

In the pilot house of their boat, Roni presented one of sixty 'homemade' Sunday school manuals to the leaders of the church in Pevas—2000.

Cory with school teacher Mommy in the houseboat living room.

Cory was actually able to man the helm for brief periods when Jim and Roni were both occupied.

Jim's Bible Institute students, some of the leaders from churches in neighboring villages—Marupa, 2000.

One of the photos of all four of the Bowers family members (and one of the best, according to Jim).

Cory's favorite sister, five-week-old Charity Lynn, and six-year-old "Snifty" who survived two bullet holes in the April 20th shoot down.

Resting in Miami Airport during Charity's first trip to Peru.

Charity takes a turn.

Roni made time for ladies and children's meetings, even after the addition of Charity to the family, as here in Aysana—Spring 2001.

In the houseboat living room—March 2001.

Hours at the helm—together, or taking turns, provided a great opportunity to talk—March 2001.

The captain had a very capable first mate— April 2001.

During a river trip with Cory's friend Getsabel—March 2001.

Cory and Charity helping mom sew—April 2001.

While interviewing Jim, Diane Sawyer also talked to Cory—May 2001.

the exorbitant import fees. This experience had provided good orientation into the bureaucratic workings of the country. Now Jim could begin assembling the materials and construct the houseboat itself.

Once again, Jim and Roni galvanized teams from their supporting churches to help in the project. Ron Reeves and Forrest Austin, both from Michigan, flew down to help Jim and one of his Peruvian friends, Omar Curmayari Aricari, fashion two giant pontoons on which the boat would (they hoped) float. The four men spent three long months welding the imported sheets of aluminum into two hulls (each one five feet deep and sixty feet long) in 100-plus-degree heat and humidity. Omar even was given the opportunity to weld although he'd never done it before.

Roni's can-do attitude helped her overlook a lot of the inherent difficulties of living in a developing country.

A steady stream of visitors passed through the Bowerses' temporary home in Andy and Di Large's enclosed property. Work teams helping to construct their houseboat, family members, groups of teens and college students on summer mission trips, all of them found hospitality—often both food and lodging—with Jim and Roni.

Jim took their visitors out on the river by speedboat. At almost every village, the routine was the same: visiting door-to-door, handing out tracts and getting acquainted with people, and introducing the visitors. They played volleyball or soccer with the local residents and talked during the break or afterward about what the tracts meant. In some places, Jim was able to hold an impromptu evening service. In such cases, the door-to-door visitation also included an invitation to the special meeting. By day's end, they were back in Iquitos, preparing for the next day's activities.

Jim and Roni purchased a refurbished World War II-vintage Willys Jeep that they used to navigate the streets of Iquitos. They were prey for the buses and trucks that barrel down the sometimes-paved roads, but they could more than hold their own against motorized tricycles (called *motocaros*), motorcycles, and pedestrians that also roam the streets.

More than one visitor expressed amazement that Roni learned to drive the old Jeep; even longtime missionaries were impressed at her ability to maneuver out into the chaotic traffic, something they never attempted in all their years on the field. She did the same with their motorcycle during the first year the Bowerses lived in Iquitos.

Roni's can-do attitude helped her overlook a lot of the inherent difficulties of living in a developing country. She frequented the open-air markets where she purchased produce, meat, and other necessities just like the locals: bargaining for the best price. She learned not to worry about the things she couldn't change (like the open sewers that ran along the sidewalks and the poverty of many of the river villages where bugs and mud were the norm) while striving to do what she could.

Roni often cooked extra food, something her mother-in-law, Wilma, had done in Brazil. She'd share it with the Manihuaris, who lived across the courtyard, or with some needy family in one of the churches. Whenever she and Jim ate out at a roadside restaurant, they made sure their leftovers went to one of the hungry children scavenging around town.

She tried to teach basic hygiene to village women, hoping to alleviate some of the diseases resulting from poor sanitation. Jim and Roni learned from Chuck and Carrie Porter to stock basic medicines, available over the counter in Iquitos: aspirin, vitamins, worm purges, and antibiotics. When they traveled on the river, they sold them to villagers well below cost or traded them for bananas or something the residents had plenty of. That way, the Peruvians would value the items (and wouldn't turn around and resell them, since they had had to pay a fee) and would enjoy improved health.

The couple constantly struggled to achieve the correct balance between giving and withholding. Jim didn't really care if someone was giving him a "sob story" or really needed his help; he'd rather err on the side of generosity and be taken in, since the Peruvians' need was greater than his whether or not it was as urgent as the supplicant claimed.

Pastor Javier remembers warning Jim that some of the supplicants were faking their need. He never forgot Jim's response: "I'd rather err by giving to someone who doesn't need it than to err by withholding from someone who really needs help."

Roni, equally touched by the plight of the poor, couldn't stand to be taken advantage of and had a hard time believing all the tragic tales, particularly when she later found some of them to be greatly exaggerated. She didn't mind helping anyone who asked, but they had better not lie to her if they expected her continued assistance, not to mention trust.

Jim and Roni came to an agreement which staved off arguments; each of them had an amount of money for which neither had to account to the other. Jim could give his sum to whomever he chose, and Roni could do likewise. Everything else they conferred on before spending, but these personal allowances could be spent without question. Each of them usually spent more than their allotted sums in helping Peruvians.

There was so much need, it was staggering; they prayed daily for wisdom to know where and how to do the most good with their time and money. What they could give was a drop in the bucket compared to the ocean of need around them. This was one of Jim and Roni's biggest frustrations with life in Peru, even though they counted it a blessing to be able to help.

It was only a few months after construction on the houseboat began that Roni felt ill. She was constantly exhausted and wondered if a full schedule in the incessant heat was taking its toll. But it was more than that; some strange and new stomach problems added to the general malaise.

Pam Hewitt, daughter of Chuck and Carrie Porter and a friend from Jim and Roni's home church in Muskegon, was visiting Iquitos with her three children at the time. Roni commented about her illness to Pam. Knowing of Roni's long struggle with infertility because the two of them had prayed about the matter for several years, Pam nevertheless told Roni, "Maybe you're pregnant."

Roni nearly laughed. "After all these years? You've got to be kidding!"

But Pam thought Roni's symptoms sounded just like her own earlier pregnancies. "I don't want to get your hopes up," she cautioned, "but I think you might want to check it out."

Almost afraid to hope, Roni bought a home pregnancy test. The results overwhelmed and exhilarated her.

"Jim, I'm pregnant!" she exclaimed. With incredible excitement, the couple discussed their imminent future. Jim, too, couldn't believe their astounding good fortune. They called their parents immediately.

"Mom, are you sitting down?" Roni asked Gloria, a favorite opening line whenever she had good news. Gloria wondered if maybe her daughter and son-in-law had decided to adopt another child; this was exactly how Roni broke the news of Cory's adoption.

Gloria was bowled over when Roni said, "I think I may be pregnant." As soon as Gloria comprehended what Roni had said, she just knew it was true. *It's a girl,* she thought to herself. She and John rushed to the store and bought a bunch of baby dresses for the granddaughter they knew Roni was carrying.

Roni welcomed with increasing elation the tiredness that signaled the advance of her pregnancy. She flew to Florida where her parents arranged for her to be seen by an obstetrician. She and Jim had waited so long for a biological child, Roni didn't want to risk anything harming this baby.

The day the doctor's office called Roni with the results of the tests, she leaped across the living room into her dad's lap, laughing and crying simultaneously. "I'm gonna have a baby! I'm gonna have a baby!" she said over and over.

Roni was nearly eight weeks along. Both she and the baby were healthy. Gloria and Roni went shopping, buying things for the baby that Roni knew she wouldn't be able to get in Peru. She didn't go all-out crazy; after all, anything she needed later on could be sent to her. But she did buy some maternity clothes and a portable crib that would fit on the houseboat. She took everything back to Iquitos in her suitcases.

Less than two weeks after returning home to the Amazon, the unthinkable happened while Jim and Roni were hosting an Expedition team, ABWE's summer program for teens seriously interested in missions. Roni was getting ready for still another group of visitors. As soon as the teens left, a construction team from Michigan would arrive to help assemble the houseboat's hull. The crew of eight would spend two weeks with Jim and Roni, putting up the boat's walls and ceilings and framing in the windows.

Jim and Roni organized and planned the two-week program and were responsible for taking the Expedition teenagers to minister in local churches. Late one night in the midst of all these activities, Roni felt sharp pains in her abdomen. She began bleeding profusely and refused to accept what she knew was happening. Hours later, Roni was lying in a hospital bed in Iquitos, having gone through a D&C to remove the tissue left by the child she'd just miscarried.

"Why?" she asked God. "Why would You give me the promise of something I've asked for over and over again, then snatch it from me? What cruelty is this?"

Although the miscarriage was a tremendous blow to Jim, he wasn't despondent the way Roni was. He hadn't carried the child in his womb for ten weeks and forged invisible bonds with the as-yet-unborn infant. He hadn't gone through the physical pain of the ordeal. He simply didn't understand how Roni felt.

The construction team that arrived less than two weeks after Roni's miscarriage knew what had happened but didn't see any signs of the emotional stress that she allowed Jim to see when they were able to be alone. The men who spent hours every day putting the boat together said, "She was always smiling." And, "She never made us feel like we were intruding."

Paula Kramer, Bill and Pat Rexford's daughter who had come to help Roni with household chores during the team's two-week stay, was at a loss. She had never miscarried. She had three daughters of her own. What could she possibly say that would ease Roni's pain one iota?

God doesn't allow anything
but what is best for each of His children.

But Roni would tell that Paula knew that sympathetic silence was exactly what she needed right then. "If you had said anything, I wouldn't have listened," Roni admitted to her friend. Paula's comfort and the loving embraces of family and friends helped in those early weeks of shock.

In fact, once the team had finished putting the houseboat's walls and seven 500-pound ceiling panels in place, Roni videotaped a walk-through of the boat. She panned across a small bedroom saying, "This is Cory's room, and a future sibling, Lord willing." That was less than a month after her miscarriage.

As she generally did, Roni turned to the pages of Scripture for answers to her current dilemma. She found particular comfort in the words of the psalmist, "He restores my soul" (Psalm 23:3a). She wrote that Psalm 77:1–15 became almost like a prayer to her:

> I cried out to God for help; I cried out to God to hear me. When I was in distress, I sought the Lord; at night I stretched out untiring hands and my soul refused to be comforted. I remembered you, O God, and I groaned; I mused, and my spirit grew faint. [Selah.] You kept my eyes from closing; I was too troubled to speak. I thought about the former days, the years of long ago; I remembered my songs in the night. My heart mused and my spirit inquired:
>
> "Will the Lord reject forever? Will he never show his favor again? Has his unfailing love vanished forever? Has his promise failed for all time? Has God forgotten to be merciful? Has he in anger withheld his compassion?" [Selah.] Then I thought, "To this I will appeal: the years of the right hand of the Most High."
>
> I will remember the deeds of the LORD; yes, I will remember your miracles of long ago. I will meditate on all your works and consider all your mighty deeds. Your ways, O God, are holy. What god is so great as our God? You are the God who performs miracles; you display your power among the peoples. With your mighty arm you redeemed your people . . .

Gloria flew to Peru to help Roni feed a second construction crew building the houseboat and to comfort her daughter. She could understand a little of what Roni was going through since she herself had miscarried around the time Roni started school and again at the age of fifty-two.

Although Roni told herself over and over in her journal and acknowledged to Jim in their conversations that God doesn't allow anything but what is best for each of His children, the loss of her unborn child threatened to undo her. She felt as if she were peering over the edge of a yawning abyss and couldn't find her way back to safe footing. She cried often and thought her son might be better off with someone else as his mother. In short, Roni was suffering from depression. And although she wasn't yet aware of it, her D&C had left her with an infected ovary.

After attempting to overcome her bleak thoughts with

strong-minded determination and the pages of Scripture which she read over and over, Roni finally realized that she needed medical help. A doctor friend in Michigan prescribed antibiotics for her infected ovary and Prozac for her bruised emotions. Both began to work quickly, healing Roni's body and soul. She was grateful that it only took a few months to regain emotional equilibrium.

Roni's inability to bear a biological child was the one trial she never completely resolved. She would always find it difficult to see women with the age her miscarried child would have been. MaryBeth Rexford gave birth to a son within weeks of Roni's due date. Little David Rexford, who gravitated to Roni in an almost uncanny manner, was a constant reminder of the child she had lost.

Roni loved Cory; he was truly hers and Jim's, and they never looked on him as second best or as a consolation prize. But in Roni's mind, bearing a child in her own body would fulfill her longing and give her greater acceptance among the Peruvian women.

Perhaps Roni didn't realize that she already held a place of high esteem among the Peruvian people. In the town of Apayacu, Hugo and Micaela Fasanando, the pastor's oldest son and daughter-in-law, were paying attention to the example they saw in Jim and Roni's life.

Micaela said, "Roni was a wise wife. She was a real help to Jim and he expressed appreciation for her. She taught the ladies to be good wives, to support our husbands, work in the church, and be involved in our husbands' ministries."

Hugo, too, recalled, "Jim and Roni had a real unity working between them. A good woman will give her husband rest. He can rely on her to help and not have to do everything himself. That's what they were like. . . . Roni always said what a good father he was and always complimented him. It made us feel strong to see their example. Jim and Roni often said, 'How can two walk together except they be in harmony?' They were in harmony. That's how they could come and serve here."

Melvina, the pastor's wife in Apayacu, said that she, too, learned from Roni's life. "She was a great example of loving the Lord first. The main thing she taught was how to treat our husbands. . . . She was a living example of the verse: 'Dear children, let us not love with words or tongue but with actions and in truth' " (1 John 3:18).

A generosity of spirit spoke volumes to the Peruvians up and down the river. Many of them said, "Everybody should be as cheerful at giving as she was."

She may not have been able to bear a biological child, but Roni's life was giving birth to spiritual offspring who watched her closely.

CHAPTER EIGHT

. . . The honor and the privilege ours;
with wounds we suffer by His side . . .

11:30 A.M., APRIL 20, 2001

"Where is Cory?" Jim asked the Peruvians. "Where is my son?"

The Peruvians attempted to placate the concerned father. "He's coming," they assured Jim. "He'll be here."

But having just suffered the unthinkable loss of his wife and baby girl, Jim wasn't satisfied. He wanted Cory with him—now. He started yelling, "I'm very concerned. Someone needs to go get him." Jim was ready to set off to find his son when Cory and the girl who had paddled the two of them to safety in the little canoe appeared through the dense undergrowth along the riverbank. Their little canoe had gone straight to the shoreline, which meant a lengthy trek through thick jungle with Cory wearing sodden clothes and nothing on his feet but socks, which seriously impeded his progress.

As Kevin and Jim had feared, the heavily crowded, double-deck riverboat pulled up right next to their canoe in Huanta's port, passengers draped over the side closest to them in an attempt to see what was going on. Jim pressed the local people to find the local medic to ride with Kevin to Pevas. That town of around eight thousand people boasted an actual clinic where Kevin's severe injuries could be treated. As fast as he was losing blood, Kevin needed immediate attention if his wounds were not to be fatal.

Jim ran up into Huanta from the port to use a radio. He contacted Rich Bracy, a pilot friend of Kevin's in Iquitos. Rich operated an air taxi in Iquitos, and his hangar stood right next to Kevin's. Rich was a personal friend as well as a fellow pilot. He started off on the emergency medical evacuation mission before Jim had finished speaking. When Jim called back to find out why the phone connection abruptly ceased, it was Rich's wife who assured Jim, "He's already on his way."

Because of his radio contact—and Jim was amazed that the equipment worked—within an hour of the shoot down, news of the incident reached ABWE headquarters and media personnel in the United States.

APPROXIMATELY NOON, APRIL 20, 2001

Using the same ham radio in Huanta, Jim phoned Bobbi Donaldson. She had known something was wrong when someone at the Iquitos tower called her every fifteen minutes from eleven o'clock on to ask, "Have you heard from Kevin yet? Have you heard from your husband?" In the midst of home-schooling her two sons, Ben, age fifteen, and Greg, age thirteen, Bobbi viewed the calls as annoying interruptions to their work.

Although the traffic controller wouldn't explain his concern, his persistent calling was unusual enough to signify that all was not well. The Donaldsons found out later that the Iquitos tower heard Kevin's frantic radio transmission, "They're killing us!"

Around noon, the same traffic controller called Bobbi once again, this time to tell her, "Rich is on his way to get Kevin."

"What?" Bobbi didn't understand what the controller meant, but he hung up before she could decipher his cryptic statement.

When Jim phoned a few minutes later, the strange events of the past hour suddenly made horrible sense. Jim said calmly, "The Peruvian air force shot us down. Roni and Charity were killed. Kevin's bleeding badly, but Cory and I are fine."

At the news of Kevin's terrible injuries, Bobbi reacted like any wife would. She screamed. Ben and Greg came running to see what was wrong. Meanwhile, Jim continued giving his report on Kevin. It was his legs, Jim explained. They were trying to evacuate Kevin from Huanta to Pevas so he could get medical help, and Rich Bracy was on the way to pick up Kevin at that very moment.

What Jim didn't know—and wouldn't for some hours—was that Rich was not on his way to Pevas. In fact, he wouldn't receive the necessary clearance to fly out of Iquitos until the next day, thanks to a bureaucratic clampdown that prevented any outsiders reaching the scene before officials sorted things out for themselves. Bobbi felt a mounting sense of frustration, helpless to reach Kevin and worried about his condition.

There was plenty to worry about. After Jim persuaded the medic in Huanta to take a look at Kevin and begin some preliminary measures, the next step was to convince the medic to accompany Kevin to Pevas. They had already decided that waiting for the *rapido,* a commercial speedboat out on the main Amazon, would take too long and use up precious time that Kevin didn't have. A small speedboat, rented from the local sawmill, could head straight to the clinic in Pevas. That was Kevin's best hope for recovery.

The reluctant medic finally agreed to accompany this patient who had dropped, literally, from the skies. They set off on the hour-and-a-half-long journey to the Pevas clinic while Jim was in town using the radio phone. The missionaries didn't even get to say good-bye or exchange messages. Jim returned to the port to find Kevin's evacuation had taken place.

The emotional setbacks of 1997 were offset by the tremendous excitement that accompanied the completion of Jim and Roni's houseboat. Once the structure was in place and most of the interior finished, they had only to wait for the Amazon River to do the rest. When the river level rose sufficiently, their boat would begin to float. Jim and Roni asked friends and supporters back in the States to pray earnestly for that day—that it would come quickly.

The houseboat had been fabricated on the property of Iquitos's yacht club, which looks nothing like the elaborate name suggests. In actuality, it's a place for boat owners to dock their vessels, eat a meal, and swim in a cordoned-off section of the Amazon. That "swimming pool" is free of piranhas and crocodiles, but several visitors noted that a snake probably could wiggle through the underwater webbing with ease.

In fact, one boatbuilding crew from Michigan had an unpleasant surprise during their two-week stay. They had been to the yacht club early in their visit to eat dinner, and they spotted an anaconda in a glass case. The constrictor was alive, which they could plainly see, and they were pleased to find it confined. On a dining excursion near the end of their trip, the Michiganders were distressed to find the glass case empty.

"Where's the snake?" Roni asked club staff members.

The nonchalant response did little to alleviate the visitors' fears. "Oh, we put it up in the rafters to take care of the rats."

The Michigan crew had seen Amazonian rats. At a church service on their first night in Iquitos, a rat "the size of a cat" pranced on a beam directly over the pastor's head. While the rest of the congregation listened intently to the message, the visitors carefully followed the rodent's progress, never taking their eyes off it for a moment.

These exciting displays of exotic wildlife weren't all that frequent. But when they did occur, Jim and Roni learned to take it all in stride like the rising and falling of the Amazon River.

With the construction of their houseboat complete, the

Bowers family actually took up residence on the boat. Jim and Roni parked their ancient Willys Jeep by a tree not too far from the boat. All they needed now was for the river to rise sufficiently for the boat to begin floating.

Jim had several contingency plans in case the boat listed to one side. Although they had done everything possible in design to allow for weight and buoyancy, it was impossible to know ahead of time what could happen. What if it sat too low on one side or the other, or was too heavy at the bow or stern? And what about the pontoons with their sealed bulkheads; what if any of them leaked? What if several of them leaked and the boat sank before their eyes?

These concerns and others made the Bowerses' prayers for safety and success all the more fervent. As the river began to rise, Jim and Roni eagerly waited each day for the water to reach their boat. They continued to make trips on the river in their speedboat.

On one such trip, Jim carefully tied the houseboat to a nearby tree that would keep the boat from drifting downriver if it began floating while they were away. When he and Roni returned to Iquitos, they rounded a bend in the river to see their boat just as they had left it—not yet floating. Roni pointed out to Jim that it was a good thing the river level hadn't risen. He'd left their Jeep parked next to the tree!

Not all the dangers the Bowers family faced were things they could prepare for. In the middle of one night, the houseboat began to shake violently. Wakened from a sound sleep, Jim and Roni thought first of a tornado, then of the possibility that the river had risen and they were being flung along the Amazon River. They eventually recognized the movement for what it was: an earthquake. Jim's mind flashed to the precariously placed logs holding up the back end of the boat. What if they fell over? The back of the boat would crash to the ground, seriously damaging the structure.

Hastily calling Cory, Jim and Roni climbed off the boat.

They could hear the excited exclamations of Peruvians from the opposite riverbank, referring to the earthquake. It confirmed what they'd already suspected. They were thankful that their boat hadn't suffered any damage.

Another night that same week, it was Jim who escaped permanent injury. He was caulking the roof of the boat, careful to keep a steady stream of sealant on the seam as he walked backward. Before he knew what had happened, he stepped off into thin air, flipping over backward, and landing on his head on the dirt nearly fifteen feet below. Roni heard him fall and ran out to find him moaning in pain, his glasses caked with dirt.

Roni used to say that one of Jim's main gifts was the gift of mercy.

After almost half an hour, Jim gradually found that he could move. With Roni's help he hobbled into the boat, his bruised neck and shoulder rapidly turning rainbow colors. Other than the tremendous headache and the stiff gait (that made the other missionaries wonder what happened to him when he arrived at their meeting the next day), Jim didn't suffer any lingering effects from that fall. An X ray showed that the scapula was intact. "I can't believe I did that," he would chide himself later. It made Roni and Jim both thankful for the many people who prayed for them every day, asking God to protect them from the dangers they faced—as well as from their own carelessness.

Jim had plenty of finish work to do on the boat. The pontoons were outfitted with a series of compartments where Roni could store supplies, medicine, books, and all the other supplies that didn't fit in her kitchen cupboards. Jim needed to do carpentry work in the kitchen and bathroom, build an extension to cover the back deck, and finish a myriad of other details (plumbing, electrical, and mechanical systems) that had been put off "until later."

His aviation maintenance training and experience in the military certainly helped Jim in building the houseboat, although he didn't have to do it completely alone. In addition to the work crews from the States who offered their expertise and muscles, Joni and Omar, brothers who attended church across the river from Iquitos, helped Jim prepare the houseboat for active duty. They also were good at helping Jim and Roni keep an eye on Cory and had a way of getting the three-year-old to practice his Spanish.

In addition to paying Joni and Omar for their services, Jim and Roni also shared their meals with the Peruvian brothers or gave them money to buy lunch in town. Jim refused to believe that the Peruvians simply were accustomed to their privations. He didn't accept the notion that they were "used to" the heat, poverty, or scarcity of food. Why shouldn't he share whatever he could? It all belonged to God anyway, and if Jim's stewardship of God's property could help anyone, so much the better. Roni used to say that one of Jim's main gifts was the gift of mercy. There was no "us" and "them" in Jim and Roni's mind; everyone was "us."

A missionary colleague said, "They treated the Peruvians like they weren't some other species. They treated them like people."

Jim and Roni's mind-set was evident to the Peruvians. Omar would say later, "They shared things with us when we didn't ask for anything. They said, 'We're here to serve you.' . . . One of the things I learned from Jim is that those who have more need to help those with less, first spiritually, then (if they have it) materially."

Teodora Sifuentes, a friend who occasionally helped Roni with extra chores, said that Roni often gave things to her. Teo recalled, "Roni said she knew that if I didn't need them, I would give them to someone who did." Peruvians in nearby towns where Jim and Roni traveled to do their ministry echoed the same sentiments: "They didn't show partiality; they were willing to help everyone."

Part of that love in action meant overlooking certain hygiene standards. Gloria couldn't get over her normally squeamish daughter hugging lice-ridden people. "She didn't let it stop her. If Roni got lice, she bought that special shampoo to get rid of them. Several times she even had to cut her hair. But that didn't stop her from treating everyone equally. She wouldn't pull back from someone who might have lice."

If Roni wasn't fastidious about her own self, she was more particular about Cory. It bothered her that the Peruvian women constantly touched him. With his sandy hair and freckled skin, Cory immediately stood out in any crowd of dark-haired, dusky Peruvians. Even as a little boy, Cory was tall for his age. His playmates tended to be children his own size, but they were several years older.

Her only child was special to Roni. She was fiercely protective of his health and safety, keeping as much harm and danger at bay as she could. She paid attention to his routine and left meetings early if she needed to get Cory in bed, but she wasn't convinced that their being missionaries meant that Cory had to put up with being pawed constantly. When he'd had enough, Roni told her son it was OK to slap the people grabbing at him.

Roni was concerned about Cory's safety. A toddler can get into plenty of trouble, even without a river for a backyard. He had strict instructions to wear a life vest at all times when on the boat's deck. It took firm reminders from both parents to make sure Cory wore the life vest as soon as his feet crossed the threshold.

One day in December 1997 while Roni was in the kitchen washing dishes, she felt the unmistakable rocking of the boat. "Jim! Jim!" she called excitedly, looking for her husband. "We're floating!" She ran out on the back deck to find Jim in the water, trying to leverage the boat off land with the gangplank. He freed the front of the boat and they were finally floating.

As the day wore on, Roni became more and more nauseated with the increasing motion of the boat. *Dear God,* she prayed, *please don't let me be sick, not after all this! How will we be able to minister to all those people on the river if I can't even travel? Please take away this nausea.* In keeping with God's gracious intervention in Roni's life, that was the last time she felt any motion sickness whatsoever.

As if that weren't enough, the houseboat floated perfectly balanced; it was completely watertight (as Jim continued to make sure by climbing down into each of the fourteen hull compartments with a flashlight). This marked a significant achievement in their first term as missionaries. Jim and Roni looked on it as their Christmas gift from God. Jim made a radio patch call to Bill Rudd in Muskegon, asking the pastor to pass on the good word: "Your prayers have been answered. The boat floats!"

All the ABWE missionaries—fifteen of them—in Iquitos joined the Bowers family for an "overnight cruise" on *El Camino* (the way), the name Jim and Roni had given their houseboat, to celebrate the start of the ministry for which Jim and Roni had been preparing themselves for more than ten years.

Living out on the river the way they did presented some strange incidents in the Bowers family's life. When they had to sign some papers for Cory's *carnet* (official residence permit), for example, the documents from Chicago reached them at the mouth of the Napo River by *rapido,* one of the speedboats that transported people between villages. The following day when Jim wanted to return the documents to Iquitos via another *rapido,* he and Cory went out into the river to flag down the boat.

Instead of stopping, it veered around them and built up speed. Jim put Cory on the front of the speedboat as he chased the *rapido,* with Cory waving to attract the attention of the faster boat. It finally slowed down, then stopped so Jim could pass on the papers. He learned that the *rapido* had been held up by pirates at this very spot not long before; hence, their reluctance to stop out in the middle of nowhere, even in broad daylight. It wasn't until those piloting the *rapido* had seen a little *gringo* boy that they were willing to stop.

Cory liked to help his dad around the boat, tying up when they arrived at a village, moving the speedboat around back, sweeping off the side, or climbing up on the roof to wash out the water tanks. Whatever his dad was doing, Cory wanted to be involved as much as he could. "It was fun for him and fun for me," Jim said. "His life on board was good. It wasn't dangerous, although any of us could have slipped and fallen . . . and drowned, but besides that, it wasn't dangerous. We taught him to stay well out of the weeds, so he was no more likely to get bitten by a snake than anybody else."

It seemed like every time they turned around, there were obstacles and problems.

Snakebites could be fatal. At one fellowship of churches in Caballococha, Jim and Andy Large and some of the local Christians had to walk through a swampy area up to their knees in water and ooze for about twenty minutes to reach the meeting site. As they walked up the riverbank to the village one man stepped on a *jergon,* a poisonous snake common to the Amazon region, which bit his ankle.

Around midnight, residents of the village came to the boat asking, "What can we do? Where can we take him?" A local medicine man had the poor victim drinking a kerosene mixture in an attempt to counteract the snake's venom, but the home remedy wasn't working. In desperation, the villagers asked Andy and Jim to use shock, a therapy they had heard of but none of them had ever tried before. Andy and Jim put leads on either side of the man's ankle and started the engine.

The night air was thick with mosquitoes, raising welts on the would be rescuers and the concerned friends as the snakebitten man writhed under the electric current. He would rest a bit before demanding, "Again." The sixty-year-old man received enough shocks that his skin was burned, as well as everything else in the vicinity of the makeshift treatment site.

When Jim and Andy left the village, they had no idea if they had hurt or helped. But the man survived, perhaps in spite of—as much as because of—their desperate measures, both men later acknowledged.

Veteran missionary Chuck Porter observed, "The strength of both Jim and Roni was the fact that when they felt that the Lord wanted them to do something, they didn't let anything stand in the way of doing it. They had so many trials that would discourage other people, like getting their stuff through customs, building the boat, and everything. It seemed like every time they turned around, there were obstacles and problems. Most people would have given up long before they got the job done. But Jim and Roni felt that this is what God wanted them to do . . . so they just carried on. They were committed to doing what God wanted them to do."

Chapter Nine

. . . And to the glory of the Lord,
those sacred scars we wear with pride. . . .

12:30 P.M., APRIL 20, 2001

Cory and Jim were ushered to a home where Cory could change out of his wet things into clean, dry clothes provided by residents of Huanta. The Peruvians bought a dress shirt, which Jim politely declined as too fancy for Cory's needs. A quick switch traded the fancy shirt for a Pokemon T-shirt (which Jim put on his son inside out) to go with the gym shorts Cory wore for the next two days. Jim wore the same fuel- and blood-soaked jeans and T-shirt he'd had on through the whole ordeal.

Roni and Charity's bodies had been carried from the canoe to the town's school building, where they were placed on a table, still draped. Jim and Cory found them by following a trail of blood drops up the sidewalk and down the porch of the long building. They could barely reach the bodies in the center of the room, as local residents packed the room. It was quite a job trying to get them out and leave the survivors in privacy. Jim and Cory hugged each other as they cried and talked about their precious loved ones.

Jim recalls not asking, "Why? Why me, God?" He was

deeply saddened, suffering greatly from the trauma and shock of all that he had gone through, but he realized that his wife and daughter were now perfectly fine. Roni had devoted her life to serving God and proclaiming the message of salvation through faith in Christ alone to those around her. Because she had placed her own faith in Jesus Christ, the moment she exited her earthly life, she entered eternal life with God. Charity, still an infant, would never have to know the emotional pain and sadness of living in a sin-filled world.

A commotion outside the school building alerted Jim that his Peruvian friends were having a hard time holding their neighbors at bay. He realized that having chased the crowd outside probably was offensive, going against local custom. Barricading the doors against them was just plain rude. He changed his mind. "Let them in," he said.

People swarmed into the room, watching the pair sitting in chairs and trying to get a look at the bodies lying under a sheet in which the local pastor and church members wrapped the bodies.

Items retrieved from the Cessna—they were floating in the water and picked up by trolling canoes—were carried piece by piece into the room. Jim arranged them on one side of the table. It was a motley assortment: Roni's purse, Cory's tennis shoes, and a charred bag containing their passports and Jim's day planner. It was inconceivable that some of the heavy things had floated. Jim opened their passports under the interested gaze of the townspeople. He wondered if the legal documents would still be useable; they just wanted to know what was going on.

One of the children crammed into the schoolroom held the orange plastic container from which Charity had been eating Cheerios minutes before the shoot down. Jim motioned to the Peruvian girl from across the room, and she brought the Tupperware container, which he added to the little pile on the table.

Everyone wanted to look under the sheets, but Jim didn't

really want everyone peering at the bodies of his wife and child. When he had to leave the room, he asked some of the women from the local church to make sure that the sheets remained in place.

EARLY AFTERNOON, APRIL 20, 2001

While talking with Cory about the fact that his mother and sister were now safe in God's care, Jim addressed the Peruvians surrounding them.

"I don't know what happened! They didn't give us any time to find out what they wanted. They just shot us." Jim explained as best he knew what had sent them from the sky into this village. He speculated that on the *frontera* (the frontier where Brazil, Colombia, and Peru all join) perhaps someone had planted drugs on the missionary floatplane and the Peruvian air force knew about it. He also spoke of forgiveness. "The pilots may have been just following orders from someone who didn't know anything," Jim told the people in Huanta.

But the grieving widower was also upset, a fact he did not try to hide. Despite his calmness, there was an underlying conviction that this never should have happened. Someone ought to have been able to prevent this needless tragedy, and that someone needed to be held accountable for Roni and Charity's deaths and Kevin's life-threatening injuries. At this moment, Jim wasn't sure if he would ever see Kevin again because of the tremendous amount of blood his colleague was losing.

Jim had made radio calls to Iquitos and to officials in Pevas; surely the Peruvian air force would return to look into the horrible mistake they had made! The missionaries had recognized the CIA plane circling overhead as they clung to the wreckage, so if all else failed, their own government surely would do something.

While waiting for outside help to arrive, Jim heard and saw an A-37—probably the very plane that shot them down—passing low and fast over the village. Peruvians scattered among the thatched-roof huts, looking for cover. They feared the plane's arrival signaled a resuming of the shooting, and Jim wasn't entirely sure that they were wrong. Cory, too, panicked at the sight of the Peruvian air force's fighter jet and fled in tears. What the jet's purpose was, no one ever knew. But after several passes at treetop level, it left without firing its machine guns, much to everyone's relief.

The first extended trip Jim and Roni made in their houseboat took place in March and April of 1998. They traveled for almost ten days, a shorter trip than they would have liked, but only one of the houseboat's two engines was functioning. The *El Camino* weighed anchor from Bellavista, the port on the Nanay River where they moored in Iquitos. During Jim and Roni's trip, they visited seven different villages.

Within fifteen minutes of leaving home port, Cory fell off a chair while helping Jim steer, cutting his lip badly in the process. Roni had anticipated trouble at the beginning of their ministry; she was just grateful it was something she was able to handle.

Jim was all set to preach in the first village where the *El Camino* stopped. People from as many as twenty churches in the "immediate" vicinity made their way to San Pedro de Falcon for the scheduled gathering. Most of the believers lived more than an hour away, even with straight-shaft motors to help power their wooden vessels.

By five in the afternoon, more than 200 people had gathered for the open-air meeting. Jim and Roni sold reading glasses for three dollars a pair and Bibles for six dollars each. Jim wrote home in an e-mail, "These are costs [the Peruvians] can somehow manage. We hope the sacrifice will help them value their Bibles more than if it was a handout."

As the evening service started, so did torrents of rain. Everyone jammed inside the school to view a video on the life of Christ, after which Jim emphasized the personal significance of Jesus' life and teachings. A discussion session starting at eleven o'clock wasn't over until the wee hours of the morning, by which time Jim's generator that powered lights and other equipment ran out of gas. So the people bedded down for the night. The schoolhouse, built on stilts, was wall-to-wall hammocks inside and below.

Jim's morning devotional was followed by the sale of more Bibles and glasses and medicines, and another meeting with church leaders. Roni taught a Bible class to more than sixty children while Jim taught the adults. Individuals taking Bible correspondence courses came to get new materials and have their homework checked. Others signed up to start their own correspondence studies: leaders with Jim, laypeople with Roni.

The busy day wasn't over until after a service that included plenty of singing—Jim taught the Peruvians new choruses, accompanied on his guitar—and was followed by *olla comun*, several large kettles filled with simmering fish, manioc root, and plantains to accompany their rice.

This church association gathering wasn't typical of Jim and Roni's routine; most often they visited congregations individually. But they enjoyed the periodic church conferences, even though it was a more structured environment.

In most towns, their routine was less frenzied. Since Jim enjoyed soccer, he played as often as possible to gain the confidence of men who were less receptive to the gospel message. Roni's motivation for joining volleyball matches was the same.

Many of the Peruvians' recollections of Roni are intertwined with volleyball games. They remember her calling out, "Who wants to play?" She coaxed those sitting around in chairs to join in and urged her teammates to give their opponents a real contest. The popular national sport was an ideal way to build friendships with local people who weren't sure how to relate to the missionary couple.

Their American visitors recognized how Jim and Roni's socializing helped them build rapport with their Peruvian neighbors. When one of the boatbuilding crews from Muskegon took on some of the locals in volleyball, they decided the teams were too unevenly matched and interspersed the Americans and Peruvians. Roni was one of the Americans assigned to the Peruvian team. "That doesn't count," the Peruvians said. "She *is* Peruvian."

Scott Schaub, only a teenager at the time, said, "Mrs. Bowers was the most skilled player on the American team, and she made up for all our mistakes and things. The term she said most was, *'deja.'* She would yell, *'Deja!'* really loud, and that's when you knew to duck because Mrs. Bowers was coming through. I found out later it meant, 'I've got it!' And that seemed to be how she took any task, any stray ball that came at her in life: *deja. God's given me this, and I'm just going to take it.*"

Jim quickly realized that many of the Peruvian pastors had little training. Educated only as far as sixth grade for the most part, the men weren't sufficiently literate to get much use out of traditional Bible study aids. Some of them had difficulty reading the Bible itself and needed to have its contents explained to them in simple language.

He loaned materials to pastors and lay leaders, creating a rotating library to assist the maximum number of people. Whenever possible, he purchased materials that he gave the men. Ernesto Flores, pastor in Huanta, is one such recipient. "Jim helped me a lot spiritually by loaning me many good Christian books and giving me some. I will never be able to repay him for the help he's been to me in my ministry," he stated.

Edwin Chavez from Aysana also relied on discipleship from Jim and materials to help him in teaching. He said, "Of all the missionaries that visited Aysana—and all of them were good—Jim and Roni were the best. They had a way of reaching people and making friends. When they came upon someone who wasn't smiling, they didn't leave him or her glum. . . . They helped everyone, not just the Christians. I received a lot of spiritual help from Jim and some good literature and teaching materials. Roni did the same thing for my wife."

Cultural factors, too, inhibited spiritual growth on a personal level. Like Native Americans, the indigenous people of South America battled daily against dependence on the alcoholic *masato,* a fermented manioc drink. The spiritual leaders fought to remain sober when all around them was the constant temptation to slip into a life of drunkenness and its accompanying troubles.

The Peruvians who trusted Christ as their Savior modeled godly living to foreigners and locals alike.

Edwin Chavez, who would eventually become the pastor in Aysana, was an alcoholic before he became a Christian and struggled to overcome his addiction even afterward. "I had a hard time because my unsaved friends were involved with alcohol, and it's a social offense to refuse the offer of a drink. But when my oldest son was two years old and I called him over to hold him, he refused. He said, 'No. You're drunk.' I thought, *If my son thinks that of me, what must my wife think of me? And the other people in the village? And God?*

"I repented of my sin and told my wife I would go forward in church to consecrate my life. . . ." According to Edwin, it was Jim's patient instruction that helped him kick his addiction for good.

Carlos Rubio Flores, a member of the Huitoto Indian tribe, also became a Christian out of a drunken lifestyle. He started out mocking Chuck Porter one afternoon after a bout of drinking, but the missionary's "calm and humble responses" completely convicted the man "within about three minutes." Carlos testified later that he knows he genuinely accepted Christ as his Savior because "the missionary said so little and I was so quickly convicted; I can see now it was the Holy Spirit working in my heart."

After his conversion, even though Carlos was "repulsed" by alcohol, overindulgence is so commonplace that he was sometimes tempted to lapse into his old ways. But reliance on God enabled him to remain clean and sober. "I have a hard time relating to people who can't conquer an addiction because my own experience was so drastic," he said. Even now, alcoholism is "the biggest obstacle" Carlos faces in the Huitoto tribe.

Another converted drunk was Juan Pedro, the man who became pastor in Santa Isabel. His drinking led to a brawl in which he pummeled a friend and left him for dead. Although the other man did not die, Juan Pedro landed in prison with serious felons and wondered how on earth he had gotten into such a fix. A Peruvian pastor came to the jail and preached on that very topic. Juan was saved, an experience he described as "feeling like a new man." The drastic change in his life is a living testimony to the power of God over sin.

The Peruvians who trusted Christ as their Savior modeled godly living to foreigners and locals alike. One man told missionary Andy Large that he read his Bible for three hours every morning. "He didn't believe me until he got up early one morning to videotape me," the Peruvian recounted. The dedication and faithfulness of men and women like these inspired others to follow their example, just as many of them had followed the example Jim and Roni set for them.

While they were teaching about godly lifestyles, Jim and Roni were discovering the practical difficulties of living on a houseboat. Managing to get up and down muddy riverbanks without incident was tricky during the daytime and could be downright hazardous at night. Water for bathing and laundry came from the murky Amazon. Deposits left by the silty river water colored all white clothing a murky beige.

Jim learned to navigate the Amazon's smaller tributaries in the houseboat. More than once, overhanging jungle scraped along the sides of the houseboat, leaving branches, sap, and thousands of ants on the roof and deck that had to be cleared off as soon as possible. One time, trees damaged the rooftop antenna that connected them by radio phone to the outside world.

Out on the river, the ham radio was their link with civilization. Roni checked in every day with Bobbi Donaldson in Iquitos. A phone patch could connect them with family and friends as far away as the United States. A supporter insisted on providing them with a satellite phone. Calls weren't cheap at three dollars a minute, but it was nice to have in order to get mechanical advice on repairing the boat engines, asking medical questions of their doctor, or hearing a familiar voice for a brief chat.

Keeping the houseboat's hulls free of floating debris that might damage the propellers meant Jim (or Roni) sometimes had to steer a zigzag path. It grew tedious on long-distance trips. Jim's GPS equipment enabled him to find any location, even in the dark, but traveling at night also meant using a spotlight to avoid hitting submerged logs in the path of the *El Camino.*

On nights when they planned a break from ministry, Jim liked to anchor near a village, or at least near people. He recognized the dangers of piracy and kidnapping, not a common threat; but it had happened from time to time, and he didn't want to give anyone an unnecessary opportunity. He equipped the houseboat with a penetrating siren. In case of emergency, that blaring noise would sound an alarm for miles around.

On one of their days off, the Bowers family didn't need to sound their alarm, but they certainly faced an emergency. Jim, Roni, and Cory had sat down to pancakes when they heard a rumbling noise. Jim looked up to see an ocean liner only a few hundred yards away. Large oceangoing vessels travel up the Amazon River periodically, and this was dangerously close. Knowing what tremendous damage the big ship's wake could inflict, Jim and Roni frantically struggled to get their anchored houseboat into a safe position.

Jim jumped into the speedboat tied at the back, reversed it, removed the rear anchor, and leaped back into the houseboat. Roni had already started the engines, so as they headed toward the front anchor and Jim pulled it out of the water, she turned the houseboat to face directly away from the waves. They were able to ride the crest, rather then be smashed by the sideways force of water. The possibility of a liner going by at night when they were asleep was a real concern and yet another item for prayer.

Because of common engine problems on their first trip, Jim had to figure out how to get into some of the treacherous ports on the riverbank with only one functioning engine. Roni often helped Jim maneuver the more ungainly houseboat by using the speedboat while Jim steered the houseboat. The teamwork that was a hallmark of this couple carried over into practically every aspect of their lives.

Many visitors recounted how Roni, hearing an infinitesimal change in the sound of the houseboat's engines, raced to the back deck, leaped into the speedboat, and threw it into reverse to keep the larger boat from getting stuck on a sandbar or to untangle it from a snarl of entrapping vegetation. Jim, in the pilothouse, could look down the length of the houseboat and see Roni in action; it got to the place where he didn't have to say anything. She just seemed to know what was needed and willingly did what she had to.

Where Jim had labored innumerable hours on the construction of their floating home, Roni spent hours making the houseboat look like a home. Visitors from the States often expressed surprise at how nice the houseboat looked. "If you didn't know it was a boat," Dan Enck observed, "you'd just think you were in an ordinary home. Roni really made it look like a home."

Roni's personal taste was stamped all over the boat, from the cheery curtains she hung over the windows, the pine country-style clothes pegs in the master bedroom, and the seasonal tablecloths she made to go under a clear plastic cover in the kitchen, to the cross-stitched pictures she hung on the walls and the throw pillows that plumped in corners of the couch. She even put sticky stuff on the bottom of her knickknacks to keep them from falling off shelves due to the boat's motion.

Making her home a haven for Jim and Cory was one of the ways Roni expressed the deep love she felt for them. Both Peruvians and Americans commented how they could easily see that she adored her husband, and Jim likewise cherished Roni.

Micaela Fasanando, a resident of Apayacu, said, "When Jim was swimming, Roni admired him. She said what a good father he was and always complimented him, building him up rather than tearing him down."

Pastor Javier Manihuari had observed the Bowers couple up close when they lived across the courtyard from him in Iquitos. "Jim would cook and help take care of Cory. He would see that Roni needed help and he would pitch in. I could see that Roni was affectionate and loving to her husband, and I would tell [my wife] Karina, 'That's what you should be for me, too.' "

Roni's journal entry on one of the few occasions when Jim had to be away, read: "Bad week—Jim gone." That's all Roni wrote for the entire time frame. She usually wrote something about each day, but as far as she was concerned, nothing of note had happened since her constant companion wasn't there to share it with.

Jim and Roni really were life partners. In a list of special memories he cherishes, Jim wrote, "We rose early together, nearly always enjoyed three meals a day together, and went to bed together every night I didn't have a late meeting. . . . She taught me to go ahead and share my true feelings at the risk of sounding dumb, to go ahead and try anything, no matter how I [thought] I might do, not to miss any opportunity."

Jim told Roni—and she, in turn, told her friends—that he would never speak ill of her to anyone. It was a trait that Roni emulated in her own life, and she advised other wives to follow suit.

For her part, Roni bragged about Jim's cleverness in having designed their floating home and often laughed at his wacky sense of humor. Jim Kramer, a friend from Muskegon, said that Roni was the only person who always laughed at her husband's antics.

"It wasn't an embarrassed laugh, and she wasn't laughing at him; she obviously thought Jim was really funny, and he'd do stuff just to make her laugh," Jim Kramer stated. Such as his magic tricks, which only Roni appeared to appreciate. One of those was balancing himself on the window ledge behind a chair to pretend he was levitating.

"Lord, show me how I can serve Jim and Cory," she wrote in her journal one day. Another entry listed those who had had an influence on her life. Roni wrote, "But I think Jim has had the biggest impact on my life. Thank You for him." She recognized that Jim could become an obsession if she wasn't careful. "Never, Lord, do I want to put anything before You, whether it be my husband . . . or anything I might want."

As determined as she was to be a good wife, Roni was equally adamant about rearing Cory properly. She marked passages in her Bible that refer to training children. Next to the verses in Luke's gospel that speak of Jesus growing "in wisdom and stature, and in favor with God and man," Roni wrote one word: "Cory." She started reading him bedtime stories and praying with him from the very beginning. She required his immediate obedience, demanded that he show respect to adults, and insisted that he learn to say "please," "thank you," and "I'm sorry." But as strict as she was, Roni always assured Cory, "Mama loves you!" He obviously recognized it, because Cory loved Roni as much as his more lenient father.

Andy Large said, "Even though we have been missionaries longer than Jim and Roni, there were things that they were doing that I wish we had been doing many years ago: getting right in and enjoying life a little more . . . and taking time with our kids."

Diane Large, too, noticed the close-knit Bowers family unit.

She described them as "a very close family, probably because they spent a lot of time together."

Another way Roni showed her love for Jim and Cory was through paying particular attention to their physical needs. She wrote out menus for every week, partly to make sure she served balanced meals, but also to aid her in purchasing supplies when she was in a place where things were available. Out on the river, she couldn't just run down to the corner store for a loaf of bread, and everything had to be made from scratch.

They made strides in relieving the people's intense spiritual emptiness.

Roni still had to improvise. If the gas oven quit working, for example, she couldn't bake. If the small solar refrigerator didn't keep things cool, she couldn't count on leftovers. Even when the fridge did work, she had to maximize every bit of space. She often went six to eight weeks between shopping trips and had to make food last in her small refrigerator, whereas women in the States who have large refrigerators can go to the store as often as they want. She used only square plastic containers and prepackaged meal-sized portions of meat so as not to waste one square inch of space.

A washing machine helped with laundry, but the dryer was simply a series of ropes strung across the back deck. It seemed that there was always something flapping in the breeze out there. The humidity kept clothes damp for a long time, and they got more than damp if Roni couldn't snatch them off the line before a storm suddenly let loose.

Jim and Roni's washing machine, usually bolted onto the back deck of their houseboat, was stolen one night and carted off by thieves in a canoe. It's obvious they didn't get far because six months later when the water receded, there sat the washing machine, rusting away.

The next piece of equipment they lost was the utility boat Jim used to cross the Nanay River from their houseboat to Iquitos. He also used it on the river to zip between neighboring towns and villages. Easier to maneuver than the 65-horsepower speedboat, the utility boat easily navigated jungle-clogged tributaries but saved time over using a canoe. The utility boat disappeared while Jim and Roni attended an annual church convention in Iquitos. Jim's tone of resignation comes through in a letter he sent to supporters back in the States.

He wrote, "I took a friend out for a couple of hours in our speedboat, looking everywhere with spotlights and asking everyone along the shore who was still awake between 11:30 P.M. and 1:30 A.M. . . . That little aluminum tender with its trusty 14-hp Johnson outboard motor was one of the most useful pieces of equipment the Lord has provided us. . . . The bigger ski boat with its 65 hp is less practical and more of a risk to leave unattended at port. Praise the Lord we do have it, and it will keep us going just fine."

Those early trips on the houseboat were memorable in many ways. Jim and Roni got a taste of what it was like to work on the river in their own home and learned a few tips from Chuck and Carrie Porter, whose responsibilities they were assuming. The younger couple saw the great needs of the Peruvian people in the towns and did what they could to alleviate physical suffering as much as they could by dispensing vitamins, aspirin, reading glasses, and cold remedies.

More importantly, they made strides in relieving the people's intense spiritual emptiness. Individuals prayed to receive Christ as Savior; some who had already trusted Christ vowed to live their lives devoted to God's leading and service, while hundreds more heard the gospel message for the first time. The Holy Spirit would work in their hearts, using the seeds planted by God's Word to grow spiritual fruit.

They were forming friendships with people along the river. Many towns recall the *El Camino* pulling into port, with Cory jumping off to help tie up the boat. Roni would sometimes call out, "Who wants to play volleyball?" And after a well-contested match, she and Jim visited houses in the village, inviting people to the evening meeting.

When they didn't play volleyball or soccer, they could spend more time counseling the Christians with needs, such as urging them to remain faithful to their spouses and maintain church attendance. Jim and Roni always asked, "How are you? What's happening in your life? Do you need anything?" One person summed it up by saying, "They made us feel special, like we were important to them."

While Jim and Roni were happy with the way the ministry was going, Jim found a few things on the boat that he needed to fix. Overall, he and Roni were pleased with how well everything worked. Surely God had aided them in the design of the structure, since neither of them had ever done anything like it before. It was an exhilarating beginning, not without difficulty or danger, but well worth all the exhausting months of planning and building.

Chapter Ten

. . . Uncertain days now echo back
that strong and urgent strain . . .

MIDAFTERNOON, APRIL 20, 2001

Police officers from Pevas arrived hours after the missionary floatplane crashed onto the Amazon, but well before the air force appeared. A speedboat from Pevas brought the police, along with members of the Peruvian army, stationed at a base there, and a reporter who wanted to interview Jim. He refused, despite one of the local Christians vouching for his reporter friend's merit.

"We've worked together before," the Peruvian told Jim. "He's OK."

But Jim declined. "I'm not talking to any reporters." It was a phrase he would repeat again and again in the coming days.

The uniformed personnel seemed to be under the charge of a young police officer. The young man began a formal interrogation of Jim. "How did this happen? What were you doing? Are you sure there were no drugs?" He also stated his intention to retain the bodies and take them back with him to Pevas.

Jim argued forcibly, "You don't understand. This is *way* bigger than you. It will go to the top level of the Peruvian government, and they'll be handling this when they get here. This has nothing to do with you or the Pevas district."

The policeman argued just as fiercely that his authority took precedence. "This is our district. This is where the incident took place, and we have to be first in the process of determining blame and what happened," he maintained.

Although Jim answered the policeman's questions, he declared, "There's no way these bodies are going to Pevas. Roni's parents will be waiting to have a funeral in the States, and as soon as we can get them there, that's where they're going. Do you have any facilities in Pevas to prepare these bodies to preserve them for several days so they can be shipped?"

No, the police officer admitted; Pevas had no such facilities. Preserving bodies in the tropics is an unknown concept. Burials take place almost immediately, within two days at the very latest.

Jim insisted that the air force would arrive at any time. "They know what they did and will come here, if for nothing else than to find what they were looking for." But as the day wore on and the air force didn't appear, Jim resigned himself to remaining in Huanta overnight and tried not to think about not being able to preserve the bodies after all.

LATE AFTERNOON, APRIL 20, 2001

The Peruvian air force finally arrived more than four hours after the shoot down of the missionary floatplane. Two Drug Enforcement Agency (DEA) agents from the United States accompanied the military to Huanta, their very presence an immediate relief to Jim, who wasn't sure if someone had planted drugs on the mission floatplane and didn't know what type of treatment to expect from the air force.

The DEA agents were surprised to find Americans waiting in Huanta. The ranking Peruvian air force officer immediately took charge, sweeping all the local residents from the schoolroom where Jim and Cory sat. They followed the crowd, not wanting to listen to the discussion about the ordeal they had miraculously survived.

For a half hour or more, Jim and Cory sat on the riverbank with their little pile of belongings. They walked up to the Peruvian air force's floatplane. The twin-engine Otter, meant to carry twenty people, was empty except for two young military men standing at the back. Jim asked them, "Do you think we'll be able to leave before dark?" If they didn't leave soon, they would have to stay the night; floatplanes can't land in the dark.

When Jim was told that he and Cory couldn't board the plane yet, they settled on a float to await their departure, their feet dangling in the water. They sat like that for quite a while before they saw a long line of people headed down the riverbank: soldiers carrying a draped stretcher, and the DEA agents.

APPROXIMATELY 5:30 P.M., APRIL 20, 2001

Jim noticed that the stretcher bearing Roni and Charity's bodies was being placed at the back of the cabin, up against the seats where he and Cory sat. Cory never looked back, so he didn't know what was going on. The DEA agents sat directly in front of Jim and Cory, with the Peruvian air force personnel and army soldiers taking the remaining seats and standing in the aisle.

The airplane, grossly overloaded, struggled to get off the water. It took a long enough time that Jim wondered if they might crash right there on the river. At that point, Jim remembers not caring at all. He wasn't the least bit concerned or afraid.

But as the floatplane finally eased into the air, Jim realized that it did matter. Cory hadn't yet accepted Christ as his Savior. Death for him—as for the rest of the occupants of the plane, Jim surmised—would not mean instantaneous reunion with God, as Roni and Charity had experienced, but eternal damnation away from God's presence.

Jim seized the moment to talk to Cory about salvation, what it means to be born sinful and, therefore, incapable of approaching

God who is holy. He talked to his son about the fact that God sent Jesus to die for the sins of the entire world, so that anyone who trusts in Christ's death as the only possible payment for sin eventually will go to heaven and live with God forever.

This was not news to Cory; his parents had shared the message of salvation with him many times, and he had heard them tell the same thing to others who had believed the message and trusted Christ as their own Savior. Unfortunately, Cory wasn't willing to do that just yet, so his father didn't pressure him.

Cory's spiritual condition gave Jim immediate focus and purpose. The fact that his son was not yet a Christian made Jim even more thankful that God had spared Cory's life. That sobering realization was enough to make Jim redirect his thoughts.

—

The *El Camino* saw a full year of usage before Jim and Roni were ready to begin their home leave. During that jam-packed twelve months, the Bowers family journeyed a dozen times on the river, sometimes as long as three months at a time, in trips that took them upriver to the borders of Brazil and Colombia. They stopped at more than fifty towns where churches had been started over the years and other towns where no one—foreign or Peruvian missionary—had ever preached before.

They learned what worked and what didn't in sharing the message of salvation through Jesus Christ. Jim and Roni found that developing peer friendships with Peruvians was a difficult task. Not only was the Peruvians' experience so different—less education, scant opportunity for obtaining possessions, and little understanding of any world but their own—but the residents along the Amazon River and its tributaries spent the majority of their lives just trying to eke out an existence.

Roni and Jim did befriend many of the Christians with whom they worked, but those relationships were mostly of the mentoring kind. As sponsors of the youth association, Jim and

Roni enjoyed the occasions when Peruvian young people traveled with them on their houseboat.

Marcos Vela, a man in his early twenties who was a leader in the youth association in Pevas, took his first trip with Jim and Roni in 1998 from Pevas to neighboring Indian villages. Marcos said, "I told Jim the problems I was going through, and he encouraged me. He said, 'You will be able to do it.' That gave me confidence and made me able to share with them. They were like parents to me. They taught me what I should be like in ministry, sharing examples of what they had done as youth leaders. I took them seriously and put into practice what they told me.

"Jim and Roni advised me to be careful in choosing a wife. They talked about what a marriage relationship should be and how to treat my spouse in the future. I saw lots of examples in their lives, especially when I traveled with them."

For peer relationships, Jim and Roni were finding that other missionaries in Peru and friends back in the States were able to fill much of that need, albeit from a distance. Connie Adams and Kay Panaggio were two new friends Roni was making in Peru. Both worked for other mission organizations. Because Connie and her family were stationed in Iquitos, the Bowers and Adams families were able to meet fairly often.

The Panaggios lived in Lima, but both families enjoyed every chance they had to get together when Jim and Roni were traveling through. They played in the park with the Panaggio children, read books, and talked. Jim encouraged the Panaggio boys in learning to play the guitar, often accompanying them on his own guitar, or he'd play soccer with them in the street.

Kay recollects, "They were very content with where they were. Jim was focused on meeting the needs out there [on the river]. He wasn't just sitting out on a boat, fishing every day. He was looking for ways to help the churches grow and help prepare the men to be better leaders.

"Roni didn't always understand everything God did, but she trusted Him. . . . I saw her resolve; she knew where she needed to be—where she wanted to be—and it was out there, using her ability to speak Spanish to share Bible stories, help the women, and all that. She wanted to be there. She had no doubt where she wanted to spend her life."

Even though Roni knew that the river work was something God had planned for her and Jim, Connie Adams understood some of the frustrations Roni faced with the lack of peer relationships on the river. "In the States, mothers who stay home all day with their children have TV and a telephone they can pick up and call their friends and family. Out here on the river, you don't have those things. You're really isolated. . . . If Roni had trouble with e-mail [they sent it out over the radio], the people in the village can't relate to the problem of the radio not working so your e-mail wouldn't send.

"Or when the walls start closing in on you, it's not like you can invite a bunch of Peruvians in to talk. They'd take one look inside your house and wonder what your problem is. We live in luxury by their standards, although by U.S. standards, we're way down there at poverty level."

They were still having to face the harsh realities of daily life in the Amazon region.

Roni and Connie swapped recipes, did tole painting, and cross-stitched or sewed together. Roni passed on to Connie tips that she had learned: how to shop for groceries for extended river trips; which merchants were honest and didn't shortchange customers; how to fix the tough-as-old-boots river chickens to make them edible.

Connie recalled, "With some people, there's a mentality that this is a hard life and it's 'sink or swim,' so you'd better learn to swim. They leave you alone to see if you can swim. Roni didn't do that. She helped me right up front."

Connie was more than willing to reciprocate in the friendship. Her older children took care of Cory when Jim and Roni wanted to go out alone; she created a pattern for Roni to make herself an outfit; she made Roni her sounding board when she herself felt stir-crazy.

Although the Bowers couple had found peer friendships, they were still having to face the harsh realities of daily life in the Amazon region. During the high-water season, many Peruvians survived on one meal a day, unable to cultivate their gardens and with nothing to trade or barter. Most people had *farinha* stored for just such a time. Even so, food was scarce and every mouthful counted.

Jim and Roni felt guilty that they were able to motor in their houseboat to towns where food was available. Even little Cory picked up on the near-starvation going on around him. The Bowerses' mealtime prayers contained extra thankfulness for the food they enjoyed. Roni and Jim shared what they could, knowing that there was no way they could feed everyone or even feed a few people as much as they needed to get them through the months of privation. Jim and Roni seized the slimmest pretext to offer food to the Peruvians, not wanting to foster an attitude of dependence on the foreigners but less willing to stand by while the gaunt children around them went hungry.

It was a tension that Jim and Roni would constantly face. *How much do we give without turning into the Great White Father? What can we do to help conditions on a broad scale? How can we facilitate the Peruvians being able to earn more income on their own? How can we get more Peruvians in the cities to reach out to their own people?*

It was a subject that they discussed with church pastors during their year of furlough in Michigan, when they reported to the churches and individuals who supported them with money and prayers. Upon landing in the States for furlough, Jim, Roni, and Cory settled into a rental property provided by Steve and Betty Schaub, former members of Calvary Church. Steve and Scott, Betty and Steve's son, were part of the Muskegon work crew that helped assemble the houseboat superstructure on-site in 1997.

The Schaubs owned several properties that they rented at very reasonable rates, including the bright blue house on Harrison Avenue that would be Jim and Roni's home for their first furlough. Heidi Enck organized renovation of the house under the supervision of Sheryl Carlisle. Other members from Calvary Church donated labor or materials to fix up the house. Jim and Roni realized how fortunate they were to have a lovely home when all they could afford was a cheap apartment.

Jim and Roni attended services at Calvary in Muskegon when Jim wasn't speaking elsewhere. Senior pastor Bill Rudd said the Bowers couple "weren't interested in self-glory." That and the fact that Jim and Roni immersed themselves in the life of Calvary Church endeared them to the rest of the congregation. They cultivated friendships with church members they had gotten to know briefly before leaving for the mission field four years earlier. Many of those relationships were strengthened during the past four years by church members' visits to Peru and via shortwave e-mails and satellite phone calls.

Jim and Roni were grateful for the way their Michigan friends embraced them. Whenever the Rexfords had a family gathering, Jim and Roni and Cory usually were included, too. They often joined in impromptu pizza parties and celebrated holidays and birthdays together. All of them recall introducing Jim and Roni to flashlight tag. Jim and Paula Kramer's wooded property provided an ideal location for this favorite after-dark activity. The Bowers family was so intent on the game, Jim and Cory even wore camouflage fatigues as they raced through the woods to avoid being "frozen" by the beam of the flashlight wielded by whoever was "it."

Roni was determined that her family experience "typical,

traditional" holiday celebrations. It was she who motivated the group into going Christmas caroling, an event they all admitted they enjoyed once they got started. She also instigated a sledding and tubing expedition that is still remembered for its hilarity.

Jim decided to take a running leap and race down the hill on an inner tube. Roni offered to hold the inflated rubber ring for him.

"Why would I let you do that?" Jim asked her. "I know you're just going to pull it away when I go to jump on it."

Roni assured him that she was trustworthy, remaining motionless as Jim feigned several rushes toward the inner tube. When he actually made his running leap, Roni jerked the tube from under him while everyone watched in gales of laughter at his exaggerated tumble down the hill.

"We all knew she was going to do it, and Jim did, too," Jim Kramer recounted. "But they were both laughing so hard and Jim played it up; you knew he was doing it for Roni."

Roni's sense of fun, combined with her organizational ability, made her a natural leader in social activities for their group of friends. She enjoyed everything immensely, whether it was playing games, swimming, or talking; and she was determined to make the most of her brief time in the States.

It wasn't as if she was obsessed with partying, though. Roni spoke to numerous ladies' groups and accompanied Jim to all their supporting churches where she talked about life in Peru.

She also took a basic medical training class in order to be able to sort out the variety of problems that appeared on her doorstep in every village on the river. She already dispensed vitamins, pain medication, oral rehydration solutions, and worm purges, and treated minor infections, dysentery, and skin disorders. However, Roni knew little else about what to do for the more perplexing conditions. She wanted to have a broader knowledge base to be of more help to the Peruvians.

One huge project Roni undertook that year was devising a plan to create Sunday school manuals for the fifty-four river towns where she and Jim ministered. They needed to be nontechnical enough to be easily used by even the least educated people but also durable. Her goal was to create fifty-two-page booklets that contained colored pictures, each with a simple lesson written on the back that Roni herself translated. Laminating the pages would make the manuals last in a place where anything that didn't mold got eaten by bugs or disintegrated within months.

But the best part of Roni's plan, and something that she and Jim often did when launching a project, was to involve the members of Calvary Church. She asked people—women primarily—to sign up to color the pages for a specific town. "Don't let your kids color these pages," she insisted. "These need to be high quality. For some of the towns, this is probably the only teaching resource they will have." Roni told the participants to pay attention to detail. "Make sure that somebody's wearing the same colored outfit on page twenty as on page one."

Like the missions-minded church it is, the people of Calvary responded with gusto. Some of the women in John and Gloria Luttig's church in Florida helped, too. Members who signed up to color booklets received a certificate that specified which town they were coloring for, in addition to the blank pages they were to color in. Most participants agreed to complete one, but a few industrious individuals signed up for two.

Each manual took hours to complete. Pat Rexford enlisted her husband's help in order to finish on time. Betty Schaub remembers the deadline for completion approaching, with dozens of pages still uncolored. "Roni kept asking, 'Are you going to finish?' I had my [teenage] daughters help me; it was getting that close."

Another of Roni's goals for that furlough year was to adopt a second child. As much as she and Jim adored Cory, they thought he needed a playmate. The family traveled so much on the river, rarely spending more than a couple of days in one place, it was hard for four-year-old Cory to make any lasting friendships. He hadn't learned a lot of Spanish and none of his playmates spoke English. His striking physical differences made him more of an outsider than a peer.

Besides which, Roni really wanted another baby, preferably a little girl. She just couldn't get it out of her head that God meant for her to bear a child. She prayed daily for one. She knew it was possible for her to conceive and regularly asked God to grant this one request.

Sure, she and Jim wanted another child, but God's timing was best.

Jim, too, thought that Cory needed someone more like himself with whom to socialize. He thought a baby girl was a good idea, although perhaps Cory would appreciate a brother more. Whoever God gave them was fine with Jim. He and Roni contacted Adoption Associates and waited for a response while they continued planning to return to the work that awaited them in Peru.

At long last, all the Sunday school manuals were collated and ready to be passed out to the river villages when Jim and Roni reached Peru. But no child had materialized for the Bowerses. It looked like they might get another boy; the birth mother had chosen them and things were in place, but they decided to leave for Peru, knowing that the young mother could change her mind during the waiting period required by law for just such a reason.

After being back in Peru for just a few weeks, Jim and Roni received word that she had done just that. They were not getting a second child after all.

"It's OK," Roni told her friends who worried how she might react. "If this is what God has for me, I can accept it."

Even though this was a disappointment for Roni, she managed to hold up better than expected. Sure, she and Jim wanted another child, but God's timing was best. They would just have to wait until He decided it was the right time for them. Their excitement about their new ministry plan kept them from dwelling on unhappy thoughts.

Kay Panaggio talked to Roni when the Bowers family stopped on their way to Iquitos. Kay wondered if her friend was mentally prepared to return to the Amazon, especially since the anticipated baby didn't materialize. "When she came through, I was a new missionary and I asked her, 'So, are you ready to go back?' And she said, 'Yep, I can't wait to get back!' " Kay thought that Roni had matured, become more settled, even though she still wanted and prayed for another baby.

"Roni shed some tears, but she wasn't devastated," Kay would say later. "She was focused and content that God had a plan. She was willing to be obedient no matter what and was eager to return to the work that they'd left."

Jim and Roni had decided that they would no longer spread themselves over fifty-plus churches on the river. Instead, they would focus on a dozen groups of Christians, teaching the leaders and strengthening the churches. Their concentrated amounts of time would enable them to see greater progress in the formative congregations. This would be a smaller sphere of influence, but it would be more effective.

The pastors of Jim and Roni's supporting churches and their mission administrator, Dave Southwell, enthusiastically endorsed their decision. Instead of doing what amounted to throwing water balloons at a forest fire, they'd be able to turn powerful fire hoses on the conflagration.

In watching Jim and Roni at work, ABWE colleague Bobbi Donaldson noticed that Roni's high expectations for herself were more realistic when it came to the Peruvian people. "Even though she was so decisive herself," Bobbi recounted, "in dealing with other people, she was very aware of their abilities and capabilities. She never demanded [anything] of them or was upset if they were unable to do what she could. She had a very good grasp of what a person was able to do. . . . Her expectations of people were always within what they could produce. The verse that says 'to whom much is given, much will be required' could be applied to her. If nothing was given, nothing was required. It's difficult when you're dealing with different people all the time and always having to be mindful of what they know."

As much as she demanded of herself, Roni squeezed every bit of pleasure she could from life. According to Bobbi, "Roni lived passionately, like every day was her last."

Chapter Eleven

. . . To count the cost, take up the cross
and join in the refrain . . .

6:00 P.M., APRIL 20, 2001

The Otter landed at the military base in Iquitos right about dark. When Jim and Cory exited the twin-engine air force floatplane, only military personnel stationed there were waiting to receive them. The DEA agents told Jim, "Come with us." Jim and Cory sat in the sport utility vehicle with dark-tinted windows for almost an hour, as Jim grew increasingly worried about the condition of his wife and daughter's bodies in the van that served as an ambulance. The air force general was summoned at Jim's request.

Jim asked the general impatiently, "What are you waiting for?" He reminded the military officer that the bodies had been sitting in the heat since eleven that morning—more than seven hours earlier—and needed to be taken to refrigeration immediately. "There's no reason for them to be sitting there. Take them to where they need to go!" Jim demanded. He had become extremely frustrated by the air force's lack of urgency that whole afternoon.

The general said, "Any minute, any minute," which turned into another twenty minutes before the Americans were allowed to leave the base. Getting past the crowd gathered at the guarded gate was surprisingly easy. The DEA agents zoomed through. "The air force gave us permission to take you to where we want," they told Jim. "We're not sure if someone will try to follow us; we're going to make sure that's not possible."

They zipped down the city streets and did some sudden, sharp turns and backtracking to shake off anyone who might be trying to follow. Jim worried that the evasive maneuvers would result in being stopped by the Iquitos police. "That will just make matters worse," he warned the DEA agents.

7:00 P.M., APRIL 20, 2001

Local police didn't stop the sport utility vehicle; they didn't even see it. Neither the media nor fellow missionaries caught a glimpse of Jim and Cory, not realizing they had just sped off in the dark vehicle. Jim and Cory were escorted, undetected, to the El Dorado hotel in downtown Iquitos.

It was something of a bittersweet moment for Jim. This four-star hotel, by far the grandest in the Amazon, was the place where Jim sometimes took Roni to eat on special occasions and where the missionaries had gathered for social events. Before returning to Michigan in March, Dave Buckley and Jim Cross had given Jim and Roni money for a getaway by themselves at the El Dorado. The couple planned to stay at the hotel in late April. Instead, Jim and Cory were staying at the El Dorado courtesy of the DEA.

The agents said, "Order anything you want from room service. We're leaving to change clothes." They gave Jim their cell phone number in case he needed to reach them. Cory thought he was hungry enough to eat French fries (a favorite), which room service sent up with a sandwich. The waiter who brought the food asked about Roni, since he had often served the couple on their dates. He couldn't believe what Jim told him. More than half of the food remained on Cory's plate; his appetite wasn't that big after all.

The phone rang. It was the local police, who were down at the El Dorado's front desk. They said, "You will have to come with us to the police station for questioning."

Visions of being detained indefinitely flitted through Jim's mind. He quickly said, "I understand that you'd want to talk to me, but the DEA agents are in charge of us. You'll need to talk with them first."

Jim immediately phoned the agents, who assured him, "We're on our way." Minutes later, one of them appeared in the hotel room. "I got rid of them for now but made arrangements for them to come here to talk to you later tonight," he said.

8:00 P.M., APRIL 20, 2001

A parade of uniformed policemen marched into Jim and Cory's hotel room. The half-dozen men, one bearing a typewriter, arranged chairs around the room. Cory soon fell asleep on the bed and slept through the entire six-hour interrogation.

This was a routine investigation of a death, the police explained to Jim. They wanted to know how Roni and Charity had died.

"They were killed by the Peruvian air force!" Jim said bluntly.

He was made to go over all the details of that day for their records. The police took breaks during the questioning, partly to accommodate the typist, who not only typed slowly but also duplicated the document by carbon paper. The process was laborious, to say the least.

10:00 P.M., APRIL 20—2:00 A.M., APRIL 21, 2001

Late Friday evening, personnel from the American embassy in Lima arrived: a senior diplomat and a Peruvian attached to the embassy. When the Peruvian saw Cory sprawled on the bed, she arranged him carefully on a pillow and covered him with a blanket. Missionary Larry Hultquist, too, sat through the questioning, then left around midnight with promises to return the next day. The police questioning lasted until 2:00 A.M., at which time everyone—police, DEA, and embassy staff—left Jim to shower and get some much-needed sleep.

Jim lay down on the bed next to Cory, gathered his son in his arms, and thought, not for the first time in twenty-four hours, how thankful he was to have Cory with him. Then somehow, despite the terrible ordeal they had just endured, he went to sleep.

Two months into their second term in Peru found Jim, Roni, and Cory on a six-week, 650-mile trip up to Brazil and Colombia, visiting all the churches where they had worked and notifying forty-some towns that, in future, the Bowers family would be available only for conferences or training seminars, not stopping by on a regular basis.

"I'm not really sure how we chose the fifteen we ended up with," Jim said later, "other than for geographical reasons. We picked a broad spectrum that included established churches and groups of Christians that were not yet organized into churches. We picked towns that we really liked, where there were people we really enjoyed, but there were others we didn't pick that we really hated to give up."

On their lengthy trip, Jim was able to e-mail reports of their progress back to Muskegon, where it was relayed among friends in supporting churches. "We plan to stop in ten towns and have at least three days with each church," Jim wrote. "But even [that] is so limited, considering how much we have to teach them of God's Word! Please pray."

Jim noticed, to his chagrin, that any kind of speed caused a wake to be thrown up into houses along the river. Since it was the high-water season, houses on stilts barely remained above the river, and sometimes it washed right up into the Peruvian people's homes.

He told Cory, "I just wasn't thinking. It's not a very good example of a considerate Christian."

"No, Daddy," Cory corrected. "They weren't thinking. They built their houses too low to the floodwater."

Flooding did present some interesting diversions, however. Traveling to churches in the speedboat sometimes meant tying the boat right up to a church itself. There also wasn't any chance of getting caught on a sandbar, a concern during low-water season.

About halfway through the trip, at the Colombian border, Jim wrote, "At about 5:30 P.M., a little before sunset . . . I shut down the port engine and got into the water to remove a fishing line from the propeller. The engine wouldn't start after that . . . it acted like it was locked up."

Jim had no choice but to proceed under power of the starboard engine only, but that left a huge trail of smoke, and the engine guzzled oil by the quarts. They were able to travel at the whopping speed of five miles per hour, something they could have achieved just floating in the current—if only they weren't traveling upstream.

As the Bowers family made their progress upriver at the speed of a casual walk, they threw wrapped candies to passing canoes, dodged fishing nets in their path, and tried to figure out a solution to their engine problem.

One of the towns where the Bowerses stopped for several days was Pevas. Jim spoke in the church and in a nearby town where he presented one of the colored Sunday school manuals so painstakingly assembled in Michigan. Roni explained to the teachers how to use the manual. Cory's contribution was to sing a duet with Jim at the conclusion of the service, even though it was late at night.

In Pevas Jim tried to repair the houseboat's engine, attempting to get the shaft out of the water sufficiently to be able to work on it. With the assistance of a dozen men, some women and children, and a couple of canoes full of water on top of logs, Jim spent three hours pushing with his speedboat. The combined efforts succeeded in raising the stern of the houseboat nearly two feet, but the shaft was still under the water. Scrapping the whole plan, they removed the logs which buckled one of the rudders, so not only did Jim have to work on the shaft underwater, he also had to remove the damaged rudder completely.

After pounding on it with a sledgehammer for an hour, Jim realized that it couldn't be straightened until he got to Iquitos. Maneuvering on the rest of the trip was much more difficult with only one rudder. This meant that Jim didn't get a break from driving, since Roni couldn't manage the extra effort of steering.

The next stop on their itinerary was Huanta. Jim and Roni's ministry on this occasion was primarily to children, since nearly every adult in town had traveled at sunrise for elections. (Heavy fines are levied against those who don't vote.) After a children's Bible lesson and a Spanish "Veggie Tales" videotape, Roni helped Jim take apart and reassemble the two engine starters to try to get at least one that would work. Five hours later, the job was done. After chatting with some of the men from the church who returned from voting, the Bowers family set off for the next town.

They picked up a hitchhiker, a woman who wanted a tow for herself and her three children in their canoe. They had quite a way to paddle in the rapidly approaching nightfall. Jim never would have found their location without his GPS equipment. As it was, he had to hope he could reach the coordinates he punched in, despite a strong current and running with only one engine, since he couldn't see anything in the ink-black darkness with no moon and a cloudy sky. Jim was pleasantly surprised by the pinpoint accuracy of the GPS, allowing him to deliver the family and make it to the next village across the main Amazon with ease.

In Apayacu, pastor Benedicto Fasanando had serious health

problems. He needed to go to Iquitos for tests and learned there that the treatment he needed was in Lima, the nation's capital. The couple debated what they should do and finally decided they ought to help. They made arrangements for the pastor and his wife, Melvina, to fly to Lima, where the pastor received treatment for his brain aneurysm.

Melvina later talked about what Jim and Roni's help meant to her family. "When my husband was ill, Jim and Roni took care of us. I had almost daily contact with them during that time . . . There's a verse that says, 'Dear children, let us not love with words or tongue but with actions and in truth' [see 1 John 3:18]. Jim and Roni were a living example of that verse."

There was no shortage of adventure.

And the family in Apayacu became some of Jim and Roni's closest friends. When he planned a surprise birthday party for Roni in July of 2000, Jim enlisted the help of the Fasanando family. He secretly made brownies—quite an accomplishment in the close confines of the houseboat—while the friends on shore made a big meal. Roni had no clue what was in store; she expected a workday, much like any other.

In addition to the meal and brownies, the surprise celebration included volleyball and a lot of laughter and conversation that the Peruvians still recall. "Roni was like a daughter born in our own house," they would repeat. "She was just like a member of our family."

While Jim and Roni were making progress with the people on their circuit, they faced the ongoing test of keeping the houseboat in running order. Jim was forever tinkering with one of the engines or the water pumps, hammering out a propeller, straightening out a shaft, or jerry-rigging some part needed to keep the boat functioning properly. He often did this while Roni drove the boat, enabling them to keep up with their schedule of meetings.

There was no shortage of adventure. Jim's toe was crushed between a log and the hull; he and Cory narrowly missed stepping on a coral snake while walking through the mud; Roni suffered a serious bladder infection; Cory had a mysterious fever that eventually disappeared.

There was even political excitement sometimes. Ecuador occasionally threatened to invade the Amazon region of Peru, despite the fact that Peru was a much bigger country. During one of Gloria Luttig's visits, Ecuador had declared its intention to bomb Iquitos and take over the city, which resulted in precautionary blackouts. But most of the time, life wasn't nearly that exotic. It consisted mostly of the routine chores of keeping house and working with people along the river.

Added to the normal challenges of daily life on a houseboat was the fact that Cory started kindergarten. Like many of her friends in Muskegon, Roni opted to home-school her son. She and Jim never considered sending Cory to boarding school, and there weren't any other alternatives.

Cory's little school desk sat in a corner of the living room, with a calendar and some of his artwork on the wall marking it as his place of study. In her organized fashion, Roni planned out lessons several weeks in advance. She tried to schedule field trips and experiments to give Cory varied experiences. They examined bugs in the jungle and on the riverbanks; they toured a bee farm, a brick factory, and the Coca-Cola bottling plant in Iquitos.

Roni home-schooled Cory in the mornings before unforeseen events prevented them from completing the day's assignments. Not that there weren't plenty of interruptions to the day as it was. Jim and Roni got up around 5:30 or so every morning in order to read their Bibles and pray. This was an activity they did together, a treasured moment of spiritual renewal at the start of each day.

After that, Roni started on breakfast, and Jim counseled the men who had already arrived at the boat to ask for his advice. If the matter seemed urgent or the need pressing, Jim dealt with the issue immediately and skipped family breakfast. Usually, he tried to wait until the meal was over to begin work.

Roni let the village women know that she was available in the afternoons. Until then, she was teaching Cory and preparing lunch. When Cory laid down for a nap, Roni was able to begin dispensing medicines, glasses, literature, Bible correspondence courses, or advice, depending on what the ladies needed from her. Since supper was the family's small meal (soup and sandwiches or something along those lines), Roni had more time to spend with the Peruvian ladies without shirking her domestic duties.

All of a sudden,
we rounded a curve and there were
about ninety people on the riverbank.

In all of her relationships, Roni was known for frank speaking. "She had soft teachings but very well put," is the way one Peruvian friend described her. One of the Americans remembers Roni talking to her about the delicate matter of weight: "I was carrying some extra pounds, and Roni made it very clear to me that she wanted me around for a long time to come." ABWE coworker Bobbi Donaldson characterized Roni as someone who was "very decisive . . . but never struck me as being insensitive."

Where Roni spoke her mind freely and sometimes had to be cautioned to think her words through carefully, Jim was more reticent. She encouraged him to share his true feelings "at the risk of sounding dumb," and to go ahead and try anything, no matter how he thought he would do, in order "not to miss an opportunity." It was simply one of the many ways in which the pair complemented one another and balanced each other's strengths and weaknesses.

Jim and Roni longed for team members, others to help them minister in the many towns along the Amazon River. Jim often explained that anyone interested in helping them needn't worry about a string of credentials but simply be a committed Christian.

"So many of the people here have been saved such a short time and have had no training at all," he explained. "The average Christian in any church in the States has lots more general Bible knowledge than anyone here and could share what they already know. They could counsel and help lead people to the Lord. That alone would be a tremendous help. If they really love the Peruvians and want to help them, there's so much they can do because . . . the Peruvians haven't been taught about most things."

Jim and Roni used themselves as a case in point; they weren't exceptional or gifted individuals. Their friend, Pam Hewitt, would repeat a similar description of them. "They were ordinary people who allowed an extraordinary God to control their lives; that made them extraordinary. There wasn't anything in them that made them better or special. I think it was God who [accomplished things] through them because they yielded to Him to a degree that is not common. It should be, but it isn't. That [yielding to God] is why they were so noteworthy."

Jim and Roni enlisted Peruvians as often as possible and encouraged visitors from the States to come and see the work for themselves. In August and September of 2000, Wilma Bowers made her first trip back to the Amazon since she and her husband had left ten years earlier.

"It was an emotional experience, seeing the jungle from the river," she said. "In all that time, Terry and I had seen it from up above." She stayed for six weeks, marveling at the way the houseboat navigated "tributaries of the tributaries" of the Amazon. "I had heard of the jungle being called a 'canopy,' but this was the first time I saw it. It was almost completely covering us as we squeezed through these little openings. You could hear the birds and the monkeys squealing. We were chugging along for hours at a time in the boat and I thought, *Where* are *we?* All of a sudden, we rounded a curve and there were about ninety people on the riverbank. They had heard us coming for hours."

Wilma said her heart melted at the sight of the Peruvians waiting to talk with Jim and Roni. "I could see how much the people loved them. I was able to watch them at work and see how God was glorified through their lives." Seeing the way her son and his family dealt with each other merely confirmed Wilma's conviction that Roni was the perfect complement to Jim, an ideal helper to him in his work, and a devoted mother to Cory. Wilma left with a new understanding and appreciation for their missionary life.

E-mail contact back to the States was sporadic, as was the satellite phone. Whenever the equipment worked and the atmospheric conditions were right, Jim and Roni enjoyed calling home and chatting with their friends. They really appreciated having e-mail through shortwave radio connection.

The Bowers family had spent the night in an isolated spot far from any town when an e-mail brought them the good news in late September that they had a baby girl, born a few weeks prematurely. "You have been linked with a birth mother who gave birth to a baby girl on September 14, 2000. . . . The baby was five pounds, twelve ounces when she was born and is in very good health," the electronic message said.

Remembering what had happened the last time she and Jim nearly became parents for the second time, Roni was scared to get too excited or share the news with too many people. Getting her hopes up only to have them dashed, or having to tell everyone, "Not this time," would be almost too much.

She wrote to her friends, "We'll try to leave by next weekend, Lord willing, so we could be there in Muskegon within a week. Wow! We are praying for the Lord's will, and we hope it's that we do get this baby in the end."

Roni had wanted a little girl, and friends of the couple thought that Jim really did, too. Perhaps this was the answer to prayer everyone had hoped for. Roni concluded her cautiously optimistic e-mail by saying, "We are excited, of course, but more than *anything* we want the Lord's will."

Roni had made a special effort to call David Rexford on September 14, his birthday. The little boy who had been a painful reminder of her miscarried child shared a birthday with the little girl she and Jim were now adopting. Roni had come full circle; from the sorrow of her loss and fighting memories, to accepting God's will, and now finally to rejoicing on what used to be such a difficult day.

Jim and Roni were due in Pevas on the day they got the e-mail about the baby girl. Jim was the guest speaker at a special conference of churches. As soon as the conference was over, the Bowers family headed back upriver to Iquitos. On that two-day journey they stopped in towns where they needed to tell the people they wouldn't be back for a while.

Although they were in a hurry to get back to Iquitos and on to the States, Jim and Roni decided it was important to keep their Sunday morning commitments in Huanta. While there, Jim told Pastor Ernesto Flores in private about the possible adoption, partly because he just wanted to share the excitement with someone, and partly because he knew that the adoption process could mean not getting back to the church for months.

Upon arriving in Iquitos, they packed up the boat and told missionary colleagues they were off to get their baby girl, Lord willing. Days later they were in Muskegon, anxiously wondering if they really were the parents of a little girl.

Chapter Twelve

. . . For should our journey lead us through the shadowlands of death . . .

7:00 A.M., APRIL 21, 2001

Jim was awakened after an all-too-brief period of sleep for more questioning, this time by the Peruvian air force. He got up, put on the same wet clothes he'd worn the entire previous day, and combed his hair. He also decided that he wasn't going to allow the air force to dominate the interrogation. He would show them how much he held them responsible for their deplorable negligence.

The air force personnel who filed into Jim's hotel room were led by a uniformed colonel who wore an enormous medal suspended on a ribbon around his neck, proclaiming his status as a judge in the proceedings. The half-dozen people filled chairs vacated just a few hours earlier by the police. The American embassy staff who sat in on the previous interviews also reappeared. Jim was grateful that the consul general himself was willing to come from Lima to be with him and Cory.

Jim's older brother, Phil, an employee of Continental Airlines, flew to Peru as soon as his mother told him about the shooting. When Phil reached Iquitos, he took Cory out of the El

Dorado so his nephew wouldn't have to sit through the long question-and-answer session.

Jim began by telling the colonel, "This interview serves no purpose. You are the ones who shot us down wrongfully, so you have no business doing the questioning. The police did a thorough job. They were here for six hours, and they're done with it."

That deliberate belligerence—Jim's predetermined orneriness—set an early negative tone for the interview. The American embassy personnel just sat silently, probably figuring their fellow citizen had a right to his anger. After a while, however, Jim began answering the questions more fully. He was actually grateful for the opportunity to talk about what had happened and to vent his feelings to the very ones responsible.

Although the air force had brought with them a laptop, the process still required frequent breaks. None of them could type well, and the person assigned to the task had to be told almost every single word, one at a time. Jim was surprised to learn later that, despite the painstakingly slow process, the air force's account was filled with factual errors.

AFTERNOON, APRIL 21, 2001

Jim lost track of who wandered in and out during the seven hours; the two DEA agents, missionary colleague Larry Hultquist, and others listened in on Jim's questioning. Once he decided to end his noncooperation protest, Jim was able to talk to his questioners and some of the U.S. embassy staff on a personal level.

The judge advocate spoke to Larry Hultquist in the hall during one break. "Is what Jim is telling us what you know as the truth in this case?" the judge asked. "It's not what I've been told by the air force." When Larry assured the judge that Jim was speaking honestly and his account could be verified by Kevin Donaldson, the judge's suspicions evaporated and he, too, became noticeably less hostile. He later stated, "I will see that the truth is set forth in this case!"

There were occasions during the questions—especially when the officers stopped for a break—when Jim had liberty to express some of his personal beliefs about God. Jim explained that his and Roni's whole purpose for being in Peru was to share with Peruvians the message of salvation from sin through Jesus Christ. Every village they visited, every home they stopped at, every person they talked to—all of it was working toward the goal of allowing Peruvians, no matter how poor or remotely located, to hear the message of hope.

As Jim explained, anyone who acknowledges his sinfulness and trusts in Christ's death alone to wipe clean the slate of sin will be saved from the otherwise inevitable fate of spending eternity in hell, banished from God's presence. Those who have trusted Christ as Savior, however, can look forward after physical death to spending eternity basking in God's presence in heaven.

The little girl they had prayed for to complete their family was now theirs.

When a person trusts Christ for salvation, God forgives his sin forever, no matter what the sin is. There is no sin too big for God to be able to forgive, just as there is no sin too small for Him to ignore. Wrongdoing offends Him equally, and we are all in need of God's forgiveness.

The recurrent theme of forgiveness boggled the minds of the Peruvian officers, who pronounced themselves perplexed. Didn't Jim want to get back at someone, anyone, just a little?

During the interview, embassy and air force personnel wrangled over whether a similar incident had occurred before. "What about that other planeload of Americans?" one embassy staff member asked. A heated discussion as to whether that plane had crashed or been shot down alerted Jim that other small planes that had simply vanished might have been made to disappear.

Jim had been told that the U.S. embassy plane would take him and Cory to Lima on the way to the States. Before leaving Iquitos, Jim wanted to go by the houseboat to get some documents and to arrange for the boat to be closed up and secured for an indefinite period of time.

Impossible as it seemed, Charity Lynn Bowers really was theirs. Jim and Roni took Cory with them to Adoption Associates near Grand Rapids, Michigan, to pick up his little sister. His parents had told Cory many times about his own adoption and what a special, incredible time it was; now he could see the process for himself as the family expanded.

Most of their friends in Muskegon decided that Jim, Roni, and Cory should have privacy for their first few days with Charity. "We'll wait until they call us," the friends agreed. "We'll just leave them alone for a while." A few of them decided there was no way they could wait; they wanted to see the answer to their prayers immediately.

Steve Schaub was one of those who appeared at the bright blue house on Harrison Street, video camera in hand, to record Charity's first day as a Bowers. His wife, Betty, refused to go along. "I could just imagine how I'd feel if anybody else barged in on me with a new baby," she admonished him. "No way am I going over there!"

Charity was asleep when Steve and the Schaubs' oldest son, Scott, appeared at the Bowerses' front door. Roni gave them strict instructions about letting her little girl continue her nap. But once they crept in and began videotaping the sleeping baby, Roni's maternal pride made her relent.

It was only the first of countless times over the following two months that Roni and Jim showed off their daughter. They poured out their love on her as they had done with Cory. The little girl they had prayed for to complete their family was now theirs. The court proceedings went through without a hitch, the paperwork they needed to complete before returning to Peru sped through official channels like greased lightning, and they introduced Charity to both of their families, not to mention the extensive church family in Muskegon.

Paula Kramer, MaryBeth Rexford, and Heidi Enck threw the baby shower at Calvary Church that literally hundreds attended. People came from Jim and Roni's supporting churches all over Michigan. "Everyone wanted to take part," Jim recalled. "So many of them had been praying earnestly that God would do this for us." Gloria Luttig said that "shower" was an appropriate term for the number of gifts that rained down: girls' clothes from infancy up to six years old, toys and books, powder and lotion. She said, "Everyone was so excited; they all wanted to give things for Charity."

Roni sorted all the clothes into piles according to size. The smaller things would be placed in the pontoon storage units on the Bowerses' houseboat in Iquitos. The larger clothes would be left with Mom and Dad Luttig to be picked up on Jim and Roni's next furlough.

This second time around at parenting, Roni was a little more relaxed. She was still strict—she couldn't not be a disciplinarian—but she seemed more comfortable at being a mother. As she had done with Cory, she began praying for Charity's spiritual development, and she asked God's help to be a good mother to both her son and daughter.

When Jim and Roni and their two children returned to Peru on January 1, 2001, they had to prepare the houseboat for travel. The never-ending repairs this time were the result of the boat having sat for several months: dead starter batteries, blown generator voltage regulator, burnt-out battery charger, and so on. Same old, same old, only more so. Jim set to work putting everything on the houseboat to rights.

Roni's parents flew down to Peru with the family, and this

was the first time John Luttig had ever seen where his daughter lived and worked. Roni wrote to Paula Kramer, "Now that he has a better idea of where we are and what we're doing, he won't be as concerned about me." She said in that same letter, "Although I'm exhausted at night, I'm quite content. I wouldn't change anything except maybe add a few more hours at the end of the day just for me. I'm enjoying this time around so much."

Jim and Roni were tired, not just from returning to the strength-sapping heat of the Amazon, but Charity wasn't sleeping well. She had begun to teethe, drooling down the front of herself and gnawing on anything she could cram into her mouth.

Late one evening a few days later, Roni e-mailed to Paula, "We decided to let her cry to see if she can go back to sleep. So far, she has only whimpered for about ten minutes (I'm very thankful for that, because I can't stand to listen to her cry) and has gone right back to sleep. The only problem is I can't seem to go right back to sleep myself."

Later that same month, Dan and Ryan Enck arrived from Muskegon for a ten-day visit. Since Jim had gotten the boat in pretty good working order, the Encks were able to see what the Bowers family's life on the river was like without Dan having to do the repairs that he planned on.

Dan and Ryan were amazed at how much the interior of the houseboat looked like, well, a home. They were impressed with Jim and Roni's generosity, shifting all the sleeping accommodations so that their guests could have their private bedroom. They were surprised—pleasantly so—by the delicious meals Roni cooked, even in the middle of nowhere. The visitors certainly could eat exotic meats like alligator or turtle if they wanted to, but they weren't living on snake eggs or anything weird like that.

Dan and thirteen-year-old Ryan wrote out abbreviated versions of their life stories and salvation experiences that Roni translated into Spanish so that when the houseboat stopped at villages along the river, Dan and Ryan could speak in the church services. Roni made the duo practice their testimonies repeatedly, giving them pointers on pronunciation and expression. She wanted them to be able to communicate clearly to the local residents and to make a favorable impression.

The scheduled trip ran into an unforeseen change of plans when Andy Large radioed early one morning to tell Jim that his houseboat had broken down somewhere downriver. He needed Jim to come and tow him back to Iquitos for repairs. Jim made abbreviated stops along the route, explaining to each village what had happened and letting them know, "I won't be able to stop until the trip back." This completely changed the nature of the Encks' time with Jim and Roni, considering that they spent many more of their days traveling in tow with the Larges and the Peruvian teenagers on Andy's boat.

Dan and Ryan had harrowing stories to send back home to Heidi and Leanne. Dan wrote in one e-mail, "Last night we were traveling from Pevas to Apayacu. We did not make it there before dark. . . . Eight of us loaded into Jim's small speedboat and took off flying through the darkness. . . . It is a rather strange feeling, speeding up the river with logs and trees coming toward you. Jim was using a spotlight to try to see.

"At one point, we passed another boat, and we all flew up in the air when we hit their wake. The spotlight went out for a few seconds, but we kept going." They made it for a two-and-a-half hour service, which was a long time for Dan and Ryan to sit in an uncomprehending stupor on unyielding wooden benches.

Ryan recalled the same adventure. "The kid on the front of the speedboat almost fell into the river when we hit that wake. Mr. Bowers hadn't been able to see because the other boat shone their light right in his eyes. . . . We kept thinking the service was almost over, but Mr. Large was saying good-bye to all the churches, and he kept telling a bunch of stories. Each one led to another one."

The Encks gained a new appreciation for the struggle of

daily living that their missionaries accepted as a matter of course. The only route from bow to stern was through Jim and Roni's bedroom, so the couple didn't have a lot of privacy. When they weren't taking foreign visitors with them—and sometimes even when they were—Peruvians traveled along. There was rarely a time when they didn't have company.

"There were bugs and mosquitoes, chiggers everywhere," Dan would say, cataloguing some drawbacks that life on the Amazon entailed. "And I'm not sure I could put up with people walking through my bedroom all the time. But Roni and Jim never made us feel as if we were an intrusion or that we were imposing on them in any way."

As Dan and Ryan pulled away from the houseboat in Jim's speedboat to catch their plane to the States, they waved to Roni and the two children standing out on the back deck. It was an image that would stick in their minds for a long time.

Early in February, Jim wrote to Michigan to ask for medical advice. Roni had a sinus infection, Cory had been running a fever for several days, and Charity had diarrhea and a runny nose. He mentioned that they had company again. A photographer was traveling along with them on their boat, gathering images for the slide library at ABWE's headquarters. It was less than a week since the Encks had left.

Jim and Roni spent the month of February taking care of final preparations to open a regional Bible institute in the town of Aysana. The idea was for leaders from surrounding towns to come for a week of training every two months. Over a period of six months, Jim led the endeavor: how to construct simple buildings, feed the students during their week of training, and find teachers willing to—and capable of—teaching Bible students.

Edwin Chavez, pastor of the church in Aysana, recounted what it was like to help plan the institute. "We had a church session with ten adults, who agreed to donate labor and as many materials from the jungle as possible, with Jim providing other funds. We started working right away on raising the first building. And we set the date for the first training session: May 1, 2001."

In addition to the Bible institute preparations, there were the usual village stops with Jim holding evening services and conducting morning Bible studies while Roni taught Cory kindergarten. Jim visited in homes during the afternoons while Roni met with the women. She found herself more limited as to what she could accomplish; it had been a while since she'd cared for a baby. Six-year-old Cory needed some supervision and often joined his dad, but Charity required almost constant attention.

Roni expressed frustration to her friends back in Michigan, wondering how much she was able to contribute directly to ministry to Peruvians at this stage of her life. She never questioned her family being her primary priority—and requested prayer for Cory's salvation—but she needed to find some outlet to touch other people's lives. She felt guilty that Jim seemed to bear that burden alone. In several journal entries, Roni prayed, "Lord, show me how I can minister. . . . These two beautiful children are a responsibility You've given me, but is there something I can do to help the people around us?"

She finally decided one way might be to allow teenaged Peruvian girls to travel with them for short periods of time. With the girls living on the houseboat and seeing how to take care of a family, have daily Bible reading and prayer times, and handle all the many demands on her time, Roni would surely be able to model a godly Christian woman's behavior if nothing else. She enjoyed putting this plan into practice.

Arodi Fasanando, the teenaged daughter of the pastor in Apayacu, described what it was like to travel with Jim and Roni. "Roni made pizza for my birthday, and that made me feel really special. It also made me feel special when she asked me to sing a duet with her in Huanta. She was very concerned that I marry someone who loves the Lord."

When Dave Buckley and Jim Cross arrived in March from

one of the Bowerses' supporting churches in Midland, Michigan, with two of their sons, the men were floored by the transparency Jim and Roni showed. During the group's first day on the boat, Roni told Pastor Buckley, "If you see anything inappropriate in our relationship to each other or to our children or in our ministry, please tell us. We want to be everything that we should."

The associate pastor wondered if he had ever encouraged that kind of involvement in his own life. "They wanted to be accountable to their churches and the people who supported them," Dave said. "But I can't remember spotting anything during that whole week. They were so conscious of doing and being what God wanted them to, I think they pretty much took care of anything as it came up."

Roni's goal was definitely to share the hope of the gospel with more people.

Jim Cross, too, marveled at the welcome he, his son, and their friends were given and the freedom to speak their minds about anything. "We didn't really know them all that well, but they made us feel as if we had been friends forever," he said.

Along with the beautiful dress his wife sent to Roni, Dave Buckley also gave Jim and Roni a little gift he'd brought along, a small book called *The Prayer of Jabez* written by Bruce Wilkinson. Dave had found it helpful and thought the couple might enjoy it. He had no idea how that little book would feature in Roni's life in the coming weeks.

She began reading the book, which elaborates on two verses found in chapter four of the book of First Chronicles in the Old Testament.

> Now Jabez was more honorable than his brothers, and his mother called his name Jabez, saying, "Because I bore him in pain." And Jabez called on the God of Israel saying, "Oh that You would bless me indeed, and enlarge my territory, that Your hand would be with me, and that You would keep me from evil, that I may not cause pain!" So God granted him what he requested. (1 Chronicles 4:9-10, NKJV).

As the author of the little book suggests, Roni began praying Jabez's prayer, asking God to bless her "indeed" and expand her sphere of influence for God's glory. Her journal indicates that she thought perhaps God's blessing might be to give her a biological child, which would be a powerful testimony to the Peruvians of God's ability to transform physical lives. That realization, in turn, might bring more Peruvians to spiritual renewal. Roni's goal was definitely to share the hope of the gospel with more people.

During the hours spent floating down the river with the visitors from Midland, Jim and Roni wondered aloud if it would be better for them to continue working on the Amazon River but instead to be based in Brazil. Cory had few friends, and as he grew older, there would be no missionary kids anywhere near his age. In Brazil, on the other hand, several missionary families had children near Cory and Charity's ages. They'd be able to grow up around other MKs but not have to be separated from their parents at boarding school. What did Pastor Dave think about that?

He told the Bowers couple that family was the first priority after God; they were right to be concerned about the welfare of their children. He didn't see that it would be any problem for their supporters; in fact, people probably would encourage the idea. Jim and Roni would have the same ministry, just in a different country.

Teenagers Jeff Cross and Jeremy Buckley never complained about the heat, the bugs, or the lack of computer access, something Jim Cross found particularly astonishing. He expected the boys to kick up a fuss, if only over the lack of technical equipment that was readily available to them in the States. Instead, they pitched in to help Roni teach children's classes, which included active games as well as a Bible lesson.

One of the games they helped Roni teach was musical benches (since there were no chairs in the town). "There are twenty-nine *niños,*" she told the children, "but only twenty-eight *caramellos.* The one who isn't able to grab a *caramello* when the music stops will sit right here next to me." Roni demonstrated by miming the recorded music and leaping up to snatch the candy she'd placed on a long bench in the center of a "circle" of benches.

She had a hard time keeping the Peruvian children from grabbing a fistful of candies when the music stopped—and from eating the candy the moment they had picked it up. Once she finally got the game going, they entered into the game with gusto.

Roni's spiritual application in Spanish was incomprehensible to her American helpers, but it was obvious the children's attention was riveted on her from the moment she arrived in their midst.

Since many of Jim and Roni's friends in the States homeschooled their children, most of the visitors on the Bowers boat were men; the women were teaching back at home. Roni encouraged Pastor Dave to return with his wife next time. "If you bring Jeannie, you can have our bed," she promised. Dave Buckley thought he and his wife might return during spring break in 2003; at least, that was the plan.

One of the last things Dave Buckley and Jim Cross did before leaving the houseboat was give Jim and Roni some money that was to be used personally, not for the ministry. "We knew if we didn't say that," Dave clarified later, "it would go straight into their work. . . . We wanted to do something for them personally." Going even further, the donors specified how the money was to be spent: Jim and Roni were to get a baby-sitter for the kids and spend a night at the El Dorado, the new four-star hotel in Iquitos, and eat a nice meal in the hotel's restaurant.

Roni started crying, and even the normally reserved Jim was visibly touched. The Bowers were appreciative whenever someone helped them—they were accustomed to doing things for others—and their gratitude only made people want to help them more.

In the middle of April, Roni phoned her parents, chatting about nothing in particular. "Are you sure there's nothing wrong? Are you sure she doesn't need anything?" Gloria asked John.

He repeated Gloria's questions to his daughter. "Your mother wants to know if you're sure you don't need anything."

No, Roni just wanted to talk. That same night, Roni called a couple of other friends, just to check in. Jim kept an eye on the clock, knowing how expensive calls back home were. Roni laughed as she cut short her conversations. "I have to hang up now, but we'll talk again soon," she promised. She planned to call back when she returned from Colombia after getting Charity's visa.

On April 17, Jim Bowers sent an e-mail to Steve Schaub. "We're finally back on-line again," he started out. The intermittent workings of electronic mail by shortwave radio could be frustrating, to say the least, since often there was no apparent reason for the cessation of service. "Things are set for our flight on Thursday morning . . . we'll go to the Peruvian consulate to take care of Charity's visa paperwork. . . . It's a two-and-a-half-hour flight, and I'm looking forward to getting a good view of our towns from the air again, as it's been a long time since we've flown with Kevin over our part of the river. I'll get a better feel for how they're situated, and their full size and location on the river."

None of them knew what lay ahead. Roni's journal entry on that day read like a prayer to God: "I'm so very grateful to have hope and to know that You are in control of every circumstance." Getting Charity's permanent residence visa seemed like such a routine matter. There was no indication to anyone that anything might go wrong, until they were blown out of the sky without warning.

CHAPTER THIRTEEN

. . . May this be our hearts' resolve
as long as we have breath . . .

AFTERNOON, APRIL 20, 2001

Dave Southwell, ABWE administrator for South America, faced the unenviable task of informing John and Gloria Luttig and Wilma Bowers that Roni and Charity had been killed. Because the preliminary information he had received was relayed thirdhand from missonary Larry Hultquist, Dave hesitated to place such a devastating call and then perhaps find out later, "It's not quite as bad as we thought."

Dave phoned Lynn Porter in Iquitos and asked her to verify the information for him. Within minutes, she called him back to confirm, "Unfortunately, it's true." Dave wanted to have as many details as possible for the families, but time was running out. If he didn't call now, as incomplete as all the information was, they'd hear it from a news broadcast, and he absolutely did not want that to happen. They deserved the courtesy of hearing from friends, even though he might wish it otherwise.

He called John and Gloria Luttig first. He phoned their church to see if their pastor or another staff member could be at the Luttig home when he broke the news, but all of them were out of town. He had no choice but to call them without a friend present to help them absorb the shock.

Gloria was at home by herself when Dave called. John was mowing lawns for one of his customers and wasn't scheduled to be home for several hours. She broke down, and as Dave tried to console her over the phone, John walked in the door. "What's wrong?" he asked his wife with obvious concern. "Nooo!" he hollered when she told him. "No!" That shock and disbelief would be echoed in Peru and across the United States again and again. It was a day that the couple would later describe as one that seemed "endless," a haze of robotic activity, friends coming and going, bringing food that the Luttigs didn't even want to touch.

Dave next phoned Dan Bowers, planning to ask him to walk down the block to his mother's house and break the news to Wilma in person. But when he called, it was Wilma who answered the phone at Dan and Amy's house. "Dan is on a field trip with his daughter at the school where Amy teaches," Wilma explained. "I'm baby-sitting my four-year-old grandson. Could I have Dan call you when he gets back?"

Dave paused for a moment, wondering what to do. But before he could speak, Wilma rushed on. "Something's happened to the plane, hasn't it?" she asked. Wilma knew that her son, daughter-in-law, and two grandchildren were scheduled to fly back to Iquitos from their brief business trip to the border. Having been a missionary pilot's wife for so many years, it was almost second nature for her to think throughout the day, "They should be at such and such a place by now."

And now, with Dave Southwell calling to talk to Dan, Wilma knew that something terrible had happened. As Dave told her the news as gently as he could, Wilma struggled to catch her breath. She knew it was true—no one would make up something so awful—but she couldn't grasp it. She just needed to sit down and catch her breath for a minute. "Are you OK?" Dave kept asking her. "Let me call someone." He was afraid that the shock had caused Wilma to suffer a heart attack. Her heart hurt terribly, Wilma would say later, but it wasn't a medical condition; it had been torn in two.

"The more publicity, the better, in a case like this."

In Apayacu among some of Jim and Roni's close Peruvian friends, the overwhelming reaction was also one of shock. Arodi Fasanando, the young woman who traveled with the Bowers family on El Camino, ran out of her house and through waist-deep flood water to her sister-in-law's house. When Arodi's mother, Melvina, returned from working in the family garden, she saw the long faces and asked, "What's wrong? Did one of the village children drown?" No, she was told, it's much worse than that. The tears shed in Peru matched those of the Bowerses' family friends in Michigan, California, and elsewhere. It just didn't seem possible that Roni and Charity were gone.

EVENING, APRIL 20, 2001

While Jim was ensconced in the El Dorado, the other ABWE missionaries in Iquitos were trying to make arrangements for the preservation of Roni and Charity's bodies. They had followed the ambulance van from the military base to the city morgue, where Larry Hultquist observed the preliminary examination and made positive identification. He and his wife Carolyn were the only ones allowed in the building.

The rest of the missionaries—Rich and Dee Donaldson, Lynn Porter, and Darlene Hull—and the Peruvian Christians gathered near the front doors were left to ask each other, "Where's Jim?" No one knew. They all assumed that Jim had traveled with the bodies to the morgue, but found that wasn't the case. The missionaries worried that Jim and Cory were being held.

Lynn Porter, one of the ABWE missionaries waiting outside the morgue, remembers trying to contact Bobbi Donaldson and wondering what to do. The group decided to go the Donaldson home while the autopsy was being performed (so they thought) on their slain colleague and her daughter. The Donaldson home was a hive of activity. Some of the local Christians and members of the international community had gathered there, taking food and waiting for updates on Kevin and the Bowerses.

At Kevin and Bobbi's house, Lynn met up with Dr. Salazar, a local Christian and friend of the ABWE missionaries, who urged the missionaries to hold a public wake. "The more publicity, the better, in a case like this," he said. By that time, Neil Heim had phoned from Lima to tell his fellow missionaries that Jim was staying at a hotel in downtown Iquitos to find out what arrangements he needed to make for people leaving the country and to gather any more facts he could pass on to ABWE mission headquarters in Pennsylvania.

While Larry Hultquist went to the El Dorado to see Jim, the other missionaries talked with Dr. Salazar about how to go about having Roni and Charity's bodies embalmed. "These people are sharks," Dr. Salazar warned Lynn. "They charge more than six hundred dollars because they know you have nowhere else to go."

As the field council treasurer, it fell to Lynn to make these arrangements. She went back to the morgue with a Christian radio announcer and Teo Sifuentes, one of Roni's friends and a member of one of the local churches. They had gathered money from the other missionaries and from ATM machines, guessing how much they would need to pay for preserving the two bodies.

The doctor had just finished his autopsy when Lynn reached the morgue some time after 10:00 P.M. She was surprised, because she thought that the autopsy was under way when she was at the morgue earlier in the evening, but she learned that the earlier procedure—whatever it was—was part of the Peruvian air force investigation.

The coroner told Lynn that the air force had tried to get him to "hush everything up" and make his report read the way they wanted it to. "But I said, 'No, I'm a doctor. I'm a professional, and I'm going to do it as I see it. I'm not going to change anything.'" He told Lynn that the embalming process would cost approximately six hundred and thirty dollars. She said she would be back in ten minutes with his money, and drove off with Teo to a secluded spot to get the money from the trunk of her car.

Once Lynn paid the doctor and obtained a receipt from him —written on a yellow sticky note, with his official seal affixed— he promised to start working immediately. He told Lynn to go to the Iquitos hospital between 7:00 and 7:30 A.M. the following morning to pick up the death certificates.

While Larry was at the El Dorado with Jim, the Donaldsons were busy trying to get Kevin back to Iquitos from Pevas. The Peruvian air force had offered to pick him up and fly him home, but Kevin refused the ride and asked instead for his friend Rich Bracy to take him to Iquitos. Kevin had his nurse phone Bobbi to say, "We need to be ready to leave the country tomorrow afternoon."

7:00 A.M., APRIL 21, 2001

Lynn Porter appeared at the hospital emergency room as instructed, met the doctor, and went with him to a side table where he wrote out the death certificates. He listed the cause of death as "homicide." He said, "It wasn't accidental. [The air force personnel] meant to shoot them. They were shooting and killed them, so it's homicide."

As soon as the coroner completed the forms, Lynn took them to the El Dorado. Larry Hultquist asked her to make copies of them and buy a pair of flip-flops for Jim, who still didn't have any shoes. Lynn bought Jim a pair of flip-flops and then went to pick up Phil Bowers at the airport and take him to the

El Dorado so he could watch Cory during the lengthy interview process.

In Huanta where OB-1408 had drifted downriver near the town's port, local people dragged it up to the riverbank and tied it there. Pastor Ernesto Flores and other Christians took turns guarding the airplane from 6:00 P.M. to 6:00 A.M. "We were afraid someone would plant drugs on the plane," he explained later. "We didn't need to watch it during the day; it was in plain sight and everybody kept their eyes on it. But at night, we kept guard to make sure nobody planted false evidence."

The two DEA agents, too, told Larry Hultquist that they intended to post guards over the downed floatplane. They were concerned about the Peruvian air force's failure to inform them that Americans had been involved in the incident, and wanted to make certain that everything was handled properly.

Peruvian air force personnel returned to the town repeatedly throughout the week, as did police officials and counternarcotics people. Extraction of the plane from the river wouldn't take place for almost a week after the shoot down, and the Christian community wanted to make sure that no one tampered with the plane in the meantime.

In the capital city of Lima, Neil Heim was wading through numerous papers, searching for forms, and handling all of the business matters relative to the airplane and the evacuation of the Bowers and Donaldson families. There were numerous practical aspects that he was involved in, mainly because the airplane was legally registered to ABEM, the organization for which ABWE missionaries work in Peru, and anything to do with the airplane had to funnel through ABEM. At the same time, ABWE headquarters had concerns to be addressed, and juggling all of these details took a great deal of time and coordination.

Having served as the business liaison previously, Neil was thankful to have the necessary background, but it had been several years since he had served in that role, and he wasn't current on all the information he needed. That changed in a hurry;

working with the military, embassy, and mission agencies almost nonstop for several weeks, Neil quickly became familiar with the details this situation entailed.

NOON, APRIL 21, 2001

After making one attempt to reach Huanta and being detained first by orders from the Iquitos tower and then by engine trouble, Rich Bracy, Kevin's fellow floatplane pilot friend, finally reached Pevas with Bobbi and flew Kevin back to Iquitos. They had to cross the river from the floating hangars on a boat, and a crowd of reporters and curiosity seekers all but clogged the path from the river up to the street as Kevin was carried by stretcher to a waiting ambulance. Bobbi climbed in with him, and they were whisked off to the Iquitos hospital. Lynn followed in her car with Kevin's parents and two sons.

At the hospital, Peruvian military personnel, U.S. embassy staff, and local media representatives all waited to talk to Kevin, who was undergoing X rays. When he hadn't come back after a fairly long amount of time, the missionaries learned he had been taken to surgery to clean out his wounds, with Dr. Salazar keeping an eye on the proceedings.

On her way to buy groceries thinking, *isn't it strange how life goes on, even in the midst of utter chaos?*, Lynn dropped Bobbi off at home to pack so the four Donaldsons could fly to Lima and on to the United States later that same day. Kevin's parents stayed with him at the hospital in case he needed anything and to make sure that the swarms of reporters didn't bother him, although the medical staff did as much as they could to thwart the efforts of persistent newshounds by moving Kevin through side entrances.

Lynn had been told to buy Coke and crackers for Kevin, since he hadn't eaten in hours and needed something in his stomach, as well as refreshments to offer the people in his room. She stopped at the store around the corner from the Donaldson home with Greg, their youngest son, to buy the food and headed back to the hospital to get the food to Kevin. As it turned out, Carolyn Hultquist had brought him Coke and crackers, and he'd already eaten those, so Lynn went back to the Donaldson home to pick up Bobbi and the bags.

LATE AFTERNOON, APRIL 21, 2001

Bobbi ran upstairs to Kevin's room, only to be told, "We were just waiting for you. We're going down to the ambulance and straight to the airport." Most of the Donaldsons' bags were still in Lynn Porter's trunk, so Lynn followed the convoy—ambulance and Rich Donaldson's truck—to the airport. She wasn't allowed out on the tarmac with the other vehicles unloading passengers and bags straight into the airplane and couldn't figure out how to get the bags to the Donaldsons. Greg was allowed to come back through security to get the rest of their luggage, and the Donaldsons left.

Everyone was crying as the speedboat took off.

In the capital city of Lima, Neil Heim's cell phone rang almost nonstop. His wife, Sandy, took calls on the regular phone line while Neil talked on the cell phone. There were so many details connected with the missionaries' hasty exodus from the country, plus all the details of deciding what to do with the mission's plane and coordinating details for the memorial services the United States embassy in Lima requested to hold on April 28.

As the mission's business manager in the capital, Neil served as a main conduit of information to ABWE's headquarters in Pennsylvania and to the United States embassy staff, as well as to his missionary colleagues up north in Iquitos. Much of what he did was to verify information being relayed to him or to find information as requested. It was a time-consuming process, but he fulfilled a vital role at a crucial time.

EARLY EVENING, APRIL 21, 2001

Omar and Joni, the brothers who assisted in building the houseboat and helped Jim with maintenance, were waiting for him at the Iquitos port when he arrived with Phil and Cory and Larry Hultquist. Without a word, the Peruvians hopped aboard the speedboat that was taking the missionaries across the river to where the houseboat was moored, wanting to be of help in any way they could, as usual.

Jim, Phil, and Cory went inside the boat with Omar and Joni; Larry stayed on the deck with the other Peruvians who were arriving, as they often did when Jim and Roni were in port. Jim hurriedly loaded two big Rubbermaid containers with a few clothes, some documents, the schoolbooks Cory would need to complete his last few weeks of kindergarten, a couple of Charity's favorite stuffed animals, and some personal photos.

Jim's last walk through the house was difficult, especially his look around Roni's kitchen. Roni, who liked to keep her house neat and clean, had—for the first time anyone could remember—gone away leaving a few dirty dishes in the sink. She never thought that anyone else would be in her kitchen before she was able to clean things up. Jim broke down. It was time to leave, and he couldn't stop crying.

Finally, he walked out the back door, locked it behind him, and handed the keys to Larry as if to say, "Here, it's yours now." He couldn't imagine ever wanting to live in it or even see it again. The houseboat had been his and Roni's dream home and ideal ministry tool, and it would forever be a reminder of everything that once was but never would be again.

Everyone was crying as the speedboat took off. Jim turned around for one last look, thinking, *This is the last time I'll see all this.*

LATE EVENING, APRIL 21, 2001

Larry planned to use his car, which was parked at the Iquitos port, to take Jim, Cory, Phil, and their things to the airport. Omar asked if he and his wife and son could go to the airport. Joni wanted to go along, too, as did the teenaged son and daughter of a close pastor friend. Then all the rest of Jim and Roni's Peruvian friends gathered there wanted to get in, but there wasn't room for everyone.

Jim pulled out some *solies,* Peruvian money, which he handed to those who couldn't fit in the car. "Take a *motocaro,*" he told them, knowing they would arrive much later but figuring the three-wheeled motorized taxis sure beat walking fifteen miles to the airport.

Once the missionaries reached the airport, they were whisked into an upstairs room, where other occupants were unceremoniously shooed out. Jim and Cory were left alone in the room, wondering what was going on. Larry was nowhere to be seen. Instead of staying upstairs alone, the Bowers pair went downstairs and found the group of about twenty-five Peruvian friends who had arrived from the port and others from the city who somehow heard of their departure. Jim and Cory had a brief chance to say farewell to them and to the remaining ABWE missionary colleagues who arrived: Rich and Dee Donaldson, Darlene Hull, and Lynn Porter.

Although Jim and Cory were leaving, Larry Hultquist would continue working on their behalf over the next several weeks, as Neil Heim was doing in Lima. The departure of the Bowerses didn't end the responsibilities for securing the mission's airplane, figuring out what went wrong, and all the other mundane details that a sudden and tragic death overseas entail for foreign residents.

A change of plans was in effect once again. Instead of traveling to Lima on the United States embassy's plane as originally scheduled, Jim and Cory would fly the usual way, on a commercial airliner. The embassy plane was going to stay in Iquitos rather than flying back to the capital city over the Andes Mountains at night.

When Jim and Cory walked out onto the tarmac to board the plane, they were stopped by passengers who had just disembarked. A United States Air Force chaplain and his wife had flown to Iquitos specially to see Jim and Cory, then learned the pair were flying out on the same aircraft they came in on. They were joined there on the tarmac by the Peruvian air force colonel who had interviewed Jim practically all day.

Still wearing his judge's medal, the Peruvian colonel again asked Jim about his faith. He wanted Jim to explain again how a person can be forgiven by God, no matter what he's done. Jim reiterated that it isn't how good or bad a person is; salvation doesn't rely on a person earning it—since none of us would be good enough to warrant it—but that it's an act of God's grace, a free gift that we don't deserve.

"I can't believe it. I've been too bad," the colonel marveled.

Jim referred to the transformation that took place in the life of Paul.

The colonel asked, "Who's Paul?"

Jim related the life story of Saul of Tarsus, an ultrazealous Jewish leader in the first century A.D. who persecuted Christians in Jerusalem. He hunted them down for capture and devised ways to have them killed. It was at Saul's feet that the men who stoned Stephen, one of Jesus' followers, laid their tunics during their gruesome task.

But one day while on his way to Damascus to kill Christians in that city, Saul encountered a blinding light and heard the voice of Jesus. He was led into Damascus where a man named Ananias explained salvation to Saul, despite his fear that Saul might harm him. Saul converted to Christianity and changed his name to Paul. Even with a new name, the man renowned for tormenting Christians had to convince his fellow believers that he was, indeed, a changed man.

He boldly preached Christianity throughout the Roman

Empire before he was imprisoned for his faith. Paul wrote a great deal of the New Testament, including the book of Romans, which is beloved for its teaching on the transforming power of God's grace in the lives of those who accept it.

Although he couldn't comprehend a faith that could so alter a person, the Peruvian air force colonel hugged both Jim and Cory, and Jim's brother, Phil, before they walked up the steps into the airliner that was waiting on them to close the doors. The seven-hour interview that had begun with near-animosity ended in an embrace. The Peruvian Christians standing upstairs in the waiting area looked down onto the brightly lit tarmac and observed Jim hugging the colonel.

On reaching the Lima airport, Jim was ushered into a private lounge, where he met up with Neil Heim. As Neil and Jim discussed last-minute business, ABWE president Michael Loftis called Neil's cell phone to talk to Jim and assure him of the office staff's prayers. The United States embassy staff facilitated Jim and Cory's departure from Peru. When customs officials said, "These passports won't work"—they had been damaged in the river after the shoot down—embassy personnel responded, "We'll make them work."

Jim and Kevin Donaldson saw each other on the airplane for the first time since they had parted in Huanta almost thirty hours earlier. It was an emotional reunion. Kevin had been through his own harrowing ordeal after leaving Huanta, losing so much blood that he nearly died before reaching medical help in Pevas. Medical teams there had been able to stabilize him and his leg, and, after a few false starts, Kevin finally had been evacuated to Iquitos. There he had surgery on his leg before being flown—with his wife and two sons—to Lima.

After they were airborne, Cory stretched out on top of Jim. Cocooned in a blanket, the two of them fell asleep for the duration of the seven-hour flight. The next thing Jim knew, a flight attendant wakened him and asked him and Cory to sit in individual seats in preparation for landing in Houston.

Chapter Fourteen

. . . I will serve the Lord. I will serve the Lord, my God.
And if God should choose and my life I lose,
though my foe may slay me, I will serve the Lord.

MORNING, APRIL 22, 2001

In Houston, Jim and Cory found waiting for them a carry-on bag filled with clothes for Cory, all donated by employees of Continental Airlines. Not only does Phil Bowers, Jim's oldest brother, work for Continental, so, too, does Roni's oldest brother, Garnett. The generous employees had spent nearly two hundred dollars on clothing. It was just the beginning of many overwhelming results of their incredible ordeal. The attention and gifts showered on Jim and Cory by well-wishers soon took on a life of their own. People wanted to express their sympathy and sorrow in a tangible way.

Jim, Cory, and Phil flew on to Raleigh, North Carolina, where Wilma waited for them. They were joined by Dave Southwell, whose job for the next few days would be to run interference for the Bowers family with the media. Everyone in print and broadcast journalism wanted to hear from Jim, but he didn't want to talk to the media until after his wife and daughter were buried. It seemed only fitting to him that he focus on this final task for them before addressing the public.

What he didn't realize and couldn't have known, since he had lived well outside the glare of media up to now, was that his very aloofness only made the press more interested in him and his story. Calvary Church in Muskegon, too, was inundated with media personnel within days of the shoot down. Pastor Bill Rudd said, "We had no idea of the scope of this tragedy, except, of course, for the Bowers and Donaldson families. . . . We didn't realize until Monday [three days after the accident] what a huge national media event this would be, and by then we were right in the middle of it."

Rudd said that not only his church members but other congregations in the area and people in the community banded together to help in whatever way they could, making sandwiches for the scores of media people that descended on the church and providing baby-sitters for the Friday night memorial service.

"I was so proud of the pastoral staff and the rest of the church body," Rudd said. "They did what a church is supposed to do: came together and functioned as a unit, without anyone ever telling them to do that. . . . I don't think we've ever had such a sense of God carrying us along."

Jim Bowers finally spoke publicly at the memorial service for Roni and Charity in Muskegon a week after their deaths. He talked of his confidence that God's hand was in this, as in all other phases of his life. "Does this seem like coincidence?" Jim asked the audience of more than one thousand, reading from a list of items proving God's divine intention. "The most significant aspect of this tragedy to me is that my son, Cory, still has an opportunity to trust Christ as his savior. We've been working on that for the past several months."

Jim offered further proof that God had a specific plan in mind on April 20, 2001. "One thing that convinces me that God did this to Roni and Charity is the profound effect this event is having on people around the world. The interest in missionary work now, I'm hoping, will result in an increase of missionaries in the future. . . . People are challenged now to go and do what

Roni did. . . . I'm convinced that God directly intervened to spare Kevin and Cory and me because He still has some kind of work for us to accomplish."

He talked about the recent events jolting complacent Christians. "I think He did that to wake up sleeping Christians, including myself, and maybe, most of all, to wake up those who have no interest in God or little interest [in Him]."

The memorial service included tributes from some of Jim and Roni's friends. Jim Kramer offered the opening prayer, saying, "Help us to understand what an incredibly committed servant Roni was, and help us to understand, too, what an incredibly great God she served."

Bobbi Donaldson called the deaths of her missionary colleague and infant daughter "a senseless tragedy." She related how Jesus Christ's death two thousand years ago seemed like a tragedy, but how thankful we all are today for what His death did for us. Jim Bowers thanked Bobbi for attending the service since her husband, Kevin, was undergoing reconstructive surgery on his leg at that very moment back in Pennsylvania. "She wanted to be there, but he wouldn't let her so she could be here," Jim said.

Pam Hewitt said that Roni's life taught "you do not always end up with the answers to your prayers that you desire, but it's OK. God is still God, and He still loves you. . . . You may not understand where He leads, but you will be safe and secure with Him anywhere. Roni's story ends where all believers' stories end: looking into the face of Jesus."

Steve Saint, son of the missionary pilot killed in Ecuador in 1956, spoke directly to Cory, talking about the confusion surrounding the death of his own father. As a young boy Steve had wondered, "Who are all these strangers talking to my mom?" Steve explained that he now sees, as an adult, how God uses even the most difficult circumstances of life to create something good.

With the death of His Son on the cross—and what could be

worse than that?—God provided the means whereby anyone can be saved. What could be better than that? From the deaths of Nate Saint and his missionary colleagues, God prompted many other people to become missionaries. Through them not only did most of the Waorani hear the gospel and become Christians, so did many other peoples throughout the world. Steve Saint himself has met scores of people who were prompted to become missionaries by learning of the life and death of Nate Saint. Steve often travels and speaks with one of the Waorani warriors who killed his father before becoming a Christian. From an apparently senseless tragedy, God created incredible victory.

Always there was that theme of forgiveness.

Elisabeth Elliot Gren, widow of Jim Elliot, one of the missionaries killed with Nate Saint in 1956, sent a recorded message to Roni and Charity's memorial service. She recounted her own loss almost fifty years earlier and how she had gone to live with the Waorani tribe that had killed her husband, taking their only child with her. Elisabeth and Valerie Elliot and Rachel Saint, Nate's sister, lived with the Waorani, translating the Bible into their language and helping to evangelize them. Many of those warriors and their families are Christians today as a result of missionaries who were unwilling to give up.

Jim Cross, who stayed with the Bowers family on their boat three weeks before Roni and Charity's death, recalled the experience for his audience. He shared Roni's statement during their first conversation on the boat. When she had spoken of some of the difficulties of living on the river and the dilemmas still ahead, Roni had told her visitors, "God doesn't owe me anything; I owe Him everything."

Jim Bowers said that knowing God planned the events of April 20 contributed to the "inexplicable" peace that he, Cory, their family, and friends all were feeling. "It may not last," he acknowledged, "but I hope it will."

Even Christians were surprised at Jim's calmness. He obviously wanted to insure that this kind of thing never happened to anyone else, but he wasn't out for blood. In fact, he said that he forgave "those who did this; those who are responsible."

Always there was that theme of forgiveness. It didn't sit well with some of his audience that Jim Bowers would so readily refuse to seek revenge. Didn't he care that gross negligence had cost the lives of his wife and daughter? Didn't he want to see Roni and Charity's deaths avenged somehow? Didn't he want to see someone take responsibility for the chain of events that snatched his wife and daughter from him?

Of course Jim cared! Of course his heart ached for himself and Cory and for Roni's family. And certainly he wanted to do everything in his power to make sure that this didn't happen to others in Peru. But was he dwelling on making those responsible pay for their mistake? No. That attitude floored the media, once they were permitted to speak with Jim. Why didn't he want retribution, they asked Jim.

The answer was easy. "How can I not forgive them when God has forgiven me so much?" Jim responded. "God has forgiven me [for my sins] and will continue to forgive me."

When Jim and Kevin sent Bibles to the Peruvian air force pilots who shot down the missionary floatplane, they wrote in the front of each one, "Forgiveness is one of the riches of God's grace."

The Peruvian consul general who attended the memorial service expressed his "deep condolences and empathy" to the Bowers and Luttig families. He said that all of Peru shared in their grief. While he didn't actually accept responsibility for the incident on behalf of his government, he did convey sorrow at the loss of innocent life.

The funeral service in Pensacola, Florida, was held at John and Gloria Luttig's church, Marcus Pointe Baptist. On that occasion, two of Roni's closest friends, Paula Kramer and MaryBeth Rexford, both talked about how much Roni meant to them.

Paula said, "While flying in Kevin's [Donaldson] plane over the villages up and down the Amazon, I heard her say as she pointed out the window, 'That's why we're here, Paula! Every one of those huts represents people who need to hear the good news.'

"Wednesday night, prior to falling asleep, I was reminded that one of Roni's goals for this year was to memorize the book of Philippians. . . . I wanted to learn what had been in Roni's thoughts over these past months. I was so encouraged when I read the verses, because they show the clear purpose behind the tragic circumstances of April 20. Philippians 1:12–14 says,

> Now I want you to know, brothers, that what has happened to me has really served to advance the gospel. As a result, it has become clear throughout the whole palace guard and to everyone else that I am in chains for Christ. Because of my chains, most of the brothers in the Lord have been encouraged to speak the word of God more courageously and fearlessly.

"Roni's death was not just another tragedy; it was clearly part of God's perfect plan to have His good news spoken 'courageously and fearlessly.' "

MaryBeth described her initial impression of Jim and Roni as "passionate Christ followers." She detailed the growth of the friendship between the two couples as she and Roni both struggled to have children. "I specifically asked God to give Roni a baby first, since I already had a child. Then I found out I was pregnant. I thought my heart would break to have to tell Roni the news."

As it turned out, Jim and Roni adopted Cory two months

before the Rexfords' daughter was born. MaryBeth explained, "You see, God answered my prayer, but not in the way I expected. Roni did receive her baby first, but initially His way of bringing His best for Jim and Roni did not *appear* best."

MaryBeth talked about Roni's miscarriage and the second adoption that nearly went through before the birth mother changed her mind, likening the incidents to unpleasantly wrapped gifts. Roni's miscarried child awaited her in heaven, and had the adoption of a second boy progressed, Roni and Jim would never have known the joy of being Charity's parents.

"God had slowly brought her through years of pain to realize that God's ways *are* best. God's heart *can* be trusted. And God *can* bring peace that passes all understanding. . . . All of us will miss Roni more deeply than can be expressed, and our hearts are filled with indescribable pain. But someday we will, together with Roni, remove the unpleasant-looking paper from all God gave us on earth and see the many unexplainable great gifts that were inside," MaryBeth concluded.

Governor Jeb Bush sent a letter that was read by his aide, Clint Furhman, and congressman Joe Scarborough addressed the congregation. The Peruvian consul general did not speak during the service, although he spoke privately with the Bowers and Luttig families before the start of the funeral.

Steve Green sang, paying tribute to the young missionary mother and daughter who lay in the single white casket at the front of the church. He had said earlier, "You lived in obscurity; you served [God] in obscurity, but you are highly favored in His sight, for 'Beautiful are the feet of those who take the gospel of good news!'" (Romans 10:15b, NIV, paraphrase).

Even though Jim, his family, and in-laws were going about the business of laying Roni and Charity to rest, attempting to retain some last shreds of privacy, there was something of a media frenzy going on. Television networks, newspapers, and magazines called ABWE's headquarters day and night with requests for interviews, with Jim preferably, but if he wasn't available, they would settle for anyone else. The Luttig and Bowers families were inundated, too; they finally quit answering their phones.

ABWE's Web site was flooded; people wanted to know all the details about the shooting down of OB-1408. They wanted to know exactly what happened and how. Many of the queries to the mission were along the lines of: Who are these people? Why would anybody want to live like that? Other questions were more searching: How could anyone think so little of possible dire consequences that they would consider it worth everything? What kind of faith did this missionary couple have? To all e-queries asking for further information on the subject of faith, ABWE sent a copy of *Anchor For the Soul* by Ray Pritchard. Nearly 300 copies of that little book were distributed by the end of June.

Reporters for print and electronic media expressed astonishment at the faith they were seeing in action. Calvary Church in Muskegon explained the gospel message to numerous reporters and distributed two books by Lee Stroebel: *Case for Faith* and *Case for Christ*. Many reporters assured the pastor that they would read the books; several have initiated ongoing conversations with Bill and Pat Rexford and others. As Pastor Rudd said, "It's as if God said, 'You media people don't know it, but I'm going to use you to get My message out to the world.'"

John and Gloria Luttig were interviewed on *Good Morning America* within days of their daughter and granddaughter's deaths. Gloria said, "I knew they were in God's hands, and I knew He would protect them. And He did, until it was time for Him to take them home. She's with Him now, and it's OK."[1]

Charlie Gibson commented to John, "Your wife expresses a faith I'm not sure many of us would have, that it's OK, given what's happened." He asked John Luttig whether he shared his wife's opinions.

"Yes, sir," John said. "There's no doubt in my mind that our daughter and granddaughter are in heaven. . . . Through it all, God is going to see us through."

When Diane Sawyer interviewed Jim for ABC's *PrimeTime Thursday* program barely two weeks after Roni and Charity were killed, she described the account as "a story of human love and suffering, and a kind of absolute faith most of us can only view from afar. Faith that sustains, even when tragedy strikes like a bolt out of the blue."[2] Diane asked Jim, "Do you wish God hadn't asked this of you? . . . What kind of God has a purpose that requires taking a baby's life?" She echoed the opinions of many who wondered how Jim could calmly say without a tinge of bitterness, "God caused this."

Jim told Diane, "I have an easy answer. . . . Even though I don't understand most of what God does, the real life isn't here on earth [but in heaven]. [Charity] had her seven months on earth, and now she's in eternity—in perfection."

In her conclusion, Diane commented that Jim wanted people to know that his faith isn't "some strange anesthetic; it consoles because it's real."

Find out what God wants you to do,
and do it with your whole heart.

Jim wondered why there was all the unabated interest in his life. Other missionaries had been killed in the course of carrying out their roles, and he hadn't seen this kind of media attention then. While he was more than happy to brag about the wife he adored—at the appropriate time—he worried that people would miss the missions purpose to which he and Roni were committed.

He heard from long-lost friends wanting to renew relationships, and total strangers expressed their sorrow at his loss. E-mails and cards arrived in an unending stream, numbering in the thousands. Concerned individuals sent him books—dozens of them—about how to cope with grief and loss. People sent all sorts of gifts: angel decorations, CDs, and hundreds of teddy bears for Cory.

Wilma Bowers and John and Gloria Luttig received expressions of sympathy from people literally all over the world. From recognized names such as Rev. Robert Schuller to former coworkers and a couple whose son and daughter-in-law were killed when the airplane in which they were flying exploded off Long Island Sound. People were gripped by this unfolding story and wanted to reach out and connect somehow to the principal players.

Jim was honored that President Bush called to express his condolences. In the course of their conversation, the President issued an invitation for Cory to visit the White House sometime "because Laura and I want to give you a hug." The father and son were scheduled to spend time with Todd and MaryBeth Rexford in the nation's capital a few weeks later, and they not only had a special tour of the White House but also visited privately with the president himself in his office.

After that meeting, Jim could phone the White House and speak to the president's assistants anytime he wanted and leave messages for George W. Bush. Even ABWE personnel phoned the presidential residence and were told, "Oh, it's you. You've got an 'advance directly to go' card."

Popular singer Gloria Estefan, meeting with the president the same day as Jim and Cory, asked to meet the Bowers pair. *Why?* Jim wondered. *Who are we?*

Requests for Jim to speak at Christian colleges, churches, and missions conferences began pouring in. That made some sense to Jim; after all, he and Roni had been involved in missions for nearly a decade. But the calls asking him to speak at events such as political fund-raisers continued to perplex Jim. "I'm just a nobody," he said. "What do I have to say that these people want to hear?"

Weeding through the invitations to speak in public, Jim accepted only a fraction. He figured that no matter what the people thought they were going to hear, there was only one thing he could say. It was the same thing he and Roni had said all their lives. Although Jim now was the only one of them remaining to say it, the message wouldn't change: Find out what God wants you to do, and do it with your whole heart. Any of you who don't know God, seek Him and find Him.

When he spoke at Piedmont Baptist College's commencement service in May, Jim urged the graduates of his alma mater to consider missions as a career. Howard Wilburton, PBC's president, decided that rather than ask for a public demonstration of how many might be willing to become missionaries, interested students should sign a paper in the administration building. More than 140 students signed their names, indicating their willingness to become missionaries.

Similar things occurred at other Bible colleges. Young people who saw the sacrifice one individual made realized that one person *can* make a difference and determined that they would do their part—whatever it was—to help people at home and overseas hear of the God who loves them and wants them to spend eternity with Him.

One of Roni's students from years back in Germany, Jennifer Kalnbach, called Jim to say that she would be going to work at the deaf school in Iquitos. Hearing-impaired herself, Jennifer learned the American Sign Language alphabet while in Germany and taught herself more sign language from books.

After graduating from college, the twenty-three-year-old said, "Lord, what do You want me to do now?" With Roni's death, Jennifer sensed God telling her, "This is where you should go; this is what I want you to do." While Jennifer was glad to go to the deaf school, she couldn't help thinking, *Miss Roni didn't have to die for me to understand that.*

Mission agencies were contacted in unprecedented numbers by people who said, "We want to share the gospel message. How do we become missionaries?" ABWE's candidate class, held each July, contained a couple who had never heard of the

Association of Baptists for World Evangelism before April 2001. When they learned of Roni Bowers's life and death, Dr. John and Beverly Tolbert asked, "What mission organization did she serve with?" John got on the Internet and found ABWE. The couple attended ABWE's missionary candidate classes, and were appointed in the class of 2001 to work with the Vietnamese in Southeast Asia.

In Cambodia, missionaries were told by a local Christian that he had been praying "for years" for the salvation of a relative, "but it wasn't until he heard about the death of Roni and Charity that he trusted Christ as his Savior."

A prison inmate in the States wrote to ABWE, saying, "I had never heard of your organization until the death of Roni and Charity Bowers in Peru. The Lord put on my heart to send a donation to their memorial fund, which I did on April 26, 2001. . . . Thank you for your wonderful work for God."

The same kinds of events were occurring all over the world and among other mission organizations. Some people confronted with the uncertainty and brevity of life wanted to make certain that if they died they would go to heaven. Others wanted to get more involved in missions efforts.

Jim and Cory began the slow process of resuming life without their wife and daughter, mother and sister. Jim moved in with his mom in North Carolina, less than a block from Jim's youngest brother, Dan, his wife, Amy, and their two children. He made frequent trips back to Michigan to see friends there and recall his and Roni's life together among those who had known her best. And he began the year of painful firsts without Roni and Charity: Roni's birthday in July, Charity's birthday in September, Cory's birthday in early November, Jim and Roni's anniversary, which fell right on Thanksgiving Day, and Christmas.

And he had to go back to the only home he and Roni had owned to pack up for good. That trip enabled Jim to visit several of the villages where he and Roni had worked, allowing their Peruvian friends to express their grief, and assuring them of his continued interest in them and their ministry. They welcomed him with—literally—open arms.

Many of them thought that they would never see Jim again after all that had happened on April 20. Doña Melvina in Apayacu said, "We thought he would just disappear. It's such an encouragement to see Jim. We can see the confidence he has in the Lord. He can show joy on his face, even though he's hurting inside. It strengthens us to see it."

Omar Curmayari Aricari expected Jim to return eventually but not until Cory was an adolescent. When he learned that Jim would be visiting only six months after the shoot down, however, he wondered what his own reaction should be. The last words he and Jim had spoken to each other were, "I'll never forget you, brother." Omar decided he should be happy, since Jim had told Pastor Javier that he was fine. Omar couldn't help his emotional reaction at seeing Jim alone. "I felt like Roni should be with him," he said.

The couple who lived across the courtyard from Jim and Roni during the time they were building the houseboat never forgot the missionaries' kindness and generosity, which they still saw in Jim's life. "The first thing Jim did was apologize for not telling us good-bye when he flew back to the States," Javier and Karina Manihuari said.

Karina recounted how Jim and Roni had invited them to the boat just a few weeks before the fatal trip. "We were all swimming," she said, "and afterward I asked Roni what all the things on the back of the boat were for—rakes, machetes, and things. She said, 'To tend my garden!' We all laughed at that."

Roni's ability to make light of her river "garden" was the sort of thing that endeared her to the Peruvians. "She was one of us," many of them said. "She loved us and accepted us."

Edwin Chavez commented, "The work they left behind; that will endure."

Every now and then, while he talked about his beloved wife, Jim's voice trailed off and his gaze grew distant, as if looking back across the fifteen wonderful years. It is then the magnitude of what happened seemed to sink in. Or, as his friends noted, when they catch themselves every time they say, "Jim and—," accustomed as they were to finishing the phrase, "—and Roni." Now it's changed to "—and Cory." It just doesn't seem right.

Jim Kramer observed that Jim Bowers isn't quite as playful anymore, not quite as mischievous. "He's lost his audience," was the conclusion. It was Roni who always found her husband's goofiness amusing, and it was for her that Jim Bowers performed. Without her around, there didn't seem to be much point.

In typical Jim fashion, he isn't bemoaning his loss. He keeps looking around him to see how he can help other people. If his painful experience could benefit others, so be it. With money being sent to ABWE for the memorial fund for Roni and Charity, there was a lot he could accomplish in Peru, even if he couldn't live there anymore. Jim decided that the memorial fund should be spent to construct a sports center in Iquitos to serve the needs of its youth. Although the young people love to play soccer, volleyball, and other sports, there are few actual playing sites. And what better way to give them hope for the future than to share the message of eternal life found in Jesus Christ?

Jim figured that if one phase of his life was over, it must be only because God had something else for him to do. And, as he had done ever since anyone can remember, he set out to find what that was. He joined an English-speaking congregation in Cary, North Carolina, where he is helping to start a Spanish-speaking church among the more than 80,000 Spanish speakers in the Raleigh-Durham area.

He also travels to Peru periodically where he is still involved with the training institute in Aysana, either helping teach or finding teachers who will instruct the men who gather for additional Bible training.

In the United States, Jim speaks several times a month, mostly close to home (while Cory attends first grade in a local

Christian school near Raleigh) but also at colleges scattered throughout the country. He pleads with those who do not yet know God personally to seek Him. "Ask Him to show Himself to you," Jim recommends. He urges Christians to shake off their complacency and follow God wholeheartedly, whatever it is He is asking them to do. We don't always understand God's plans, Jim acknowledges, but we can still accept them and continue to obey God, no matter what He chooses to bring into our lives. And he echoes the words Roni spoke so often to friends and stated to Jim Cross and Dave Buckley in late March of 2001: "God doesn't owe me anything; I owe Him everything."

Appendix A

Text of speech Jim Bowers gave at the memorial service for Roni and Charity Bowers in Fruitport, Michigan, on April 27, 2001.

I want to thank all of you who've prayed for Cory and me during these past eight days. You've been so good. You've prayed and helped in so many meaningful ways. It's just unbelievable how so many people have come around us and been there for us.

We're overwhelmed by the e-mails. I just took a little time last night to read 100 or so of them, and it was so encouraging. Some people didn't know what to write and others knew exactly what to write. Once in a while I came across an e-mail from someone who knew Roni. That was very encouraging, the things they had to say helped remind me of her.

A lot of you have called, too. I'm sorry for those I haven't been able to answer and also those e-mails I certainly won't be able to answer for some time; I'll be reading them for a while yet. But thank you so much!

You've done a good job in assuring us—Cory and me—that you love us. We know that you love us. Many of you traveled a long distance to be here tonight. I'll have to mention at least one who came. One of Roni's best friends came from Russia to be here tonight. Thank you, Toni.

I want to start off by thanking those who were on the scene that first day. Sorry you can't be here tonight; maybe you're watching by television. First of all, my good friend and excellent pilot who is in surgery right now. And while I'm at it, I'd better thank Bobbi. She's here. She wanted to be there, but she couldn't be because Kevin wouldn't let her. She's here. Thank you, Bobbi, for those wonderful words, too. We're praying for you, Kevin. You all can stop praying for me now for a minute and pray for Kevin, OK? He's in surgery right now and apparently he's a little late in coming out. He has lots of surgeries ahead. I look forward to seeing him soon.

I also want to thank our friends in Huanta; and the police in Pevas nearby, who were the first officials on the scene; and the Peruvian air force, who were there about four hours later. Maybe since this is taped, I could just thank them directly.

I also want to give special thanks to the DEA agents God sent on that plane to be with us. They didn't know why they were going, but they were a welcome sight. They gave us a sense of safety amongst the Peruvian officers, and protection and also comfort. They were surprised to see us.

I also want to thank the U.S. embassy personnel and the ambassador for all that they did. They just took care of us.

I might as well say thanks to Continental Airlines for giving us the red-carpet treatment at their expense. Thank you.

And to all our dear friends: You've made this as smooth as possible right from the very first gunshot. What can I say? Thank you.

Most of all I want to thank my God. He's a sovereign God. I'm finding that out more now. Some of you might ask, "Why thank God?" Of course, now after hearing some people speak tonight, you're realizing why, maybe. Could this really be God's plan for Roni and Charity; God's plan for Cory and me and our family? I'd like to tell you why I believe so, why I'm coming to believe so. I didn't believe that at all during the incident of the tragedy, or the day or two after that. But I began to see some things and God's hand at work. I'll let you come to your own conclusions.

I have a list here, and this is a partial list—it's less than half, because of time. But I'd like to read a list of things, and you tell me if this was of God or not. Of course, there could be some coincidences, but you tell me (with this half a list) if that could've been a coincidence.

- Of the many bullets that penetrated the aircraft, not one of them hit Cory or me. Despite the fact that one of the first ones made a big hole in the windshield in front of my head, coming from behind. None of them incapacitated Kevin completely.
- The fire extinguisher worked, as some on my boat don't, and it worked exceptionally; I was very surprised. Without it, we all would have died.
- Roni and Charity were instantly killed by the same bullet. (Would you say that's a stray bullet?) And it didn't reach Kevin, who was right in front of Charity; it stayed in Charity. That was a sovereign bullet.
- Neither Cory nor I were afraid. Can you believe that? We didn't scream out or yell. We were able to react quickly and think clearly throughout the entire event, as was Kevin.
- Despite major damage to Kevin's legs, he was still able to bring us to safety on the river, even though we were far from the river when it happened.
- I had just enough time—and just enough strength—to get Roni and Charity out of that aircraft before it went underwater.
- And although we floated in the river for quite a long time, a canoe came just before it was too late.

- We were shot down right over a town of witnesses, which helped at the very beginning, and some of them were very good friends of mine.
- Incredibly, the town had a radio on which we were able to call for help. That's very unusual. And the radio worked. And my calls on that jungle radio to Kevin's wife, Bobbi, at home, caught her at home; she answered the phone. Kevin's pilot friend was at home, also, and ready to fly to get him that very instant.
- And the three of us who survived—can you believe this? we're very fortunate—we have no sense of guilt for responsibility for Charity and Roni's death, as would be the case if we had been careless or negligent somehow. And it's a great relief to me.
- Both Cory and I are experiencing inexplicable peace right now. Many have told me that won't last, but I'm praying that it will.
- Another incredible thing: our attitude toward those responsible for this—my attitude, Cory's attitude, Kevin's attitude, the attitude of our families, many of our friends, and many Christians around the world (and you can see their attitude)—it's different, isn't it? I'm not bragging about my attitude. God's given me peace.
- Also, one thing that convinces me that God did this to Roni and Charity, is the profound effect this event is having on people around the world. The interest in missionary work now, I'm hoping, will result in an increase of missionaries in the future. I'm sure it will; people are challenged now to go and do what Roni did.
- And most of all, those of you who are parents, the most significant aspect of this whole tragedy is that my son, Cory, still has an opportunity to trust Christ as his Savior. We've been working on that for the past few months. Many of you have prayed for Cory, and we're still praying. God spared him. Keep praying.

And, of course, there's lots more. Maybe some other time you'll hear the other details; some of them are even better.

I'm convinced that God directly intervened to spare Kevin and Cory and me, because He still has some kind of work for us to accomplish. I think He did that also to wake up sleeping Christians, including myself, and maybe most of all, to wake up those who have no interest in God (or little interest). And I say tonight: Wake up! I have a new perspective, of course.

I'd like to shift my focus briefly away from these events of last Friday to some personal recollections of my wife and Charity.

We knew Charity as a precious gift from God; that was our main feeling about her. Those of you who held her and played with her most recently and saw her when she was older will agree with Cory and me that Charity was as perfect as any baby could be. She was beginning to crawl. She was picking herself up in her crib and on the chair. She was getting everywhere. I had to make some special arrangements for the doors so she couldn't get out. She had her first tooth. Charity and Cory were having a race to see whose tooth would come in quickest.

Many of you have been helping to take care of Charity, sending formula from the States. I calculated she's had over a barrel of formula: 60 gallons. That's a lot. She was growing and, compared to the Peruvians, very chubby but very healthy. She was the delight of all the Peruvians along the river. It was fun to show her off, and they just loved holding her.

I have lots to say about Roni. People tonight have said great things about her. And on the television, I haven't had a chance to see, but they're saying, "Everybody's talking about Roni."

But what's interesting, and you'll all agree, those of you who know her, you'd still be saying many of the same things about her even if she were here tonight, if you had the chance. I suppose you're all making up for me not bragging enough about her. Those of you who knew Roni know how special of a person she really was. I was grateful I knew her even more, and I know that she's even more incredible than you may have thought. I was the fortunate one to have her, though I certainly did not deserve her.

I'd like to say some things about Roni that might be interesting to you. She was, to me, an excellent coworker. I would have liked to have another man to travel the river with, to be a team, but that wasn't possible. . . . We worked together. Not only did she care for my needs, as that was her main ministry, but we worked together . . . as a beautiful team. And she was used greatly of the Lord to help me in the ministry. She was a wise counselor, many times without even knowing it. And I suppose I have to thank my in-laws for that. They taught her many things that affected me. And, most of all, she was my best friend. I'm happy to say that tonight.

Some other things that you'll all agree about Roni: She was very loving. She tried to accept everyone, no matter what they were like. She worked at that and helped me with that. She was grateful; she had little interest in possessions. (She would have to, to live on a boat. She planned to, for the rest of her life in the jungle.)

She was very humble, not interested at all in receiving recognition for anything. She was preoccupied with always doing what was right in God's eyes. Even though she didn't always live up to that, it was a big concern of hers and a big example for me to follow. Roni taught me so much, and I've often wondered what I would be like if not for her example.

Roni did several things well. She wasn't all that talented as far as many people would say in the world's ways, but she was in some very special ways.

She was incredibly consistent in her loving discipline of Cory from the very beginning. . . . She was a good person, so her parents must have been very consistent in discipline. She gave 100 percent of herself to Charity. She thanked God for that gift every single day.

She was an excellent schoolteacher. I listened to her and tried my best not to annoy them and to bother them, although I got in the way a lot. But she was very consistent and serious. She was concerned that Cory get a good education.

And she was a very effective teacher of the Peruvian children, helping the Peruvian women understand biblical truth better. They absolutely loved her. It's very hard for them tonight. We heard that many of them are making the long trip from their villages to be there tonight at the memorial [in Iquitos] that's going on right now. Many more things I could say, of course.

I'd like to say a little bit about us, about Roni and me. A couple of months ago, I decided it was time to make a list again, a list of all Roni's good qualities that would help me start complimenting and encouraging her more frequently. What I'm telling you tonight are things she's heard me say before; of course, not as often as I should have. And I thank God that He gave me that opportunity before it was too late. God put that on my heart to make that list. I'm very grateful for that.

It was very obvious to both of us that God brought us together, and many people who knew us at the beginning of our marriage would say the same thing. During our fifteen years together, our relationship steadily grew closer and stronger.

And we were fortunate to have received good counsel during that first year of marriage. The counsel was this: In order to have a successful marriage, we needed to learn to put God first (or to love God more than we loved each other). It sounded silly at first. We worked at it.

And it may sound strange to some of you, but our most enjoyable times together—Roni would say this, too—in recent years were the early mornings we spent praying and studying the Bible. In fact, we found our wake-up time gradually getting earlier and earlier because we enjoyed that time so much together. It became a significant part of our life and our relationship.

I'll cherish Roni's Bible and her journal; they're full of personal notes to herself and to God. And I pray that God will often bring those things to mind, those good insights that Roni shared with me so often. They were very special. I only wish I had written more of them down. I miss her!

Now, what will the future hold? What will I do now? Life will continue to be difficult without Roni and Charity. I will miss not seeing Charity doing all the things I expected to enjoy, and I certainly will miss Roni's wise counsel, godly example, and many other things.

It seems pretty obvious to me that God has chosen Cory and me to represent Him in a bigger way, a lot bigger than I would have imagined. I'm sure God wants me to serve Him in a new way now; only He knows. As another missionary wrote (the apostle Paul, who encouraged me with these words, as he did his original readers): "When I am weak, then I am strong." Meaning, I don't feel equipped to do this new ministry, whatever it might be, but I'm glad for that. Because that's when God can really use me His way, and I'm looking forward to it.

Humanly speaking, Roni and Charity's deaths were exactly what Bobbi said: absolutely senseless. Wouldn't you think they should be one of the last ones to be shot to death? You know, that's comforting to me. Some of you might think I'm crazy. I know—I'm learning—that God's ways are sometimes, and even often, inhuman. How could something so terrible be so good? Of course, I could say that now, and next month it may be quite different. But I believe the truth: Many good things have happened, and many more are to come.

Some might be wondering, "What good has happened, and what good is there to come out of this? There's nothing good about this." Although in my ministry experience . . . I found that God gets most people's attention by allowing them to experience some kind of crisis. . . . It wakes us up. Of course, this is not a crisis for Roni.

Before you start to think that Roni's some supersaint, I lived with her, so I know better. Some people, maybe some people watching on TV, would think, "Well, that's great. You know she's in heaven; look how she lived. Sounds like she was some superperson, wasn't she?" And, yes, she was.

"So, therefore, it's obvious she's in heaven. Who could've lived better than Roni? I sure can't! So that's why we know she's in heaven," some might say. God didn't say that.

What would Roni want me to say tonight? I've been trying to think of that. I'd like this to be her night and to say what she would have said.

One thing I want you to know: Roni has forgiven the pilot who shot her. She's forgiven . . . whoever might have made their mistake, and so should I. And I have. How could I not when God has forgiven me so? God will continue to forgive me no matter what I do because of Christ.

Those people who did that simply were used by God. Whether you want to believe it or not, I believe it. They were used by Him, by God, to accomplish His purpose in this, maybe similar to the Roman soldiers whom God used to put Christ on the cross.

I think Roni would say to believers tonight, those of you who know the fact that God's Son, Jesus Christ, died on the cross. But more than that, you've decided to leave that in God's hands. You've said, "God, Jesus' death is good enough for me. I don't deserve to know You; I don't deserve to go where You are, because I was born a sinner, separated from You. But You provided a way, and I trust that. I'm trusting in that way, which was Christ's sacrifice. He died for me." That's what Roni lived. She believed it with all her heart. And that's why I know she's in heaven. . . . So what would she say to you fellow believers, you, her brothers and sisters tonight, here in Muskegon, and those of you around the world? What would she say to you? . . . I think she would say, "Wake up, those of you who are sleeping spiritually."

I'm sure she has a different perspective now, doesn't she? I wondered at first how could she not be sad for Cory and me? She's not. She knows that our suffering and our struggles are temporary. And they're very brief, compared with [eternity] when everything's perfect. . . . I'd still think she would be worried about us, but she's not; she knows how it ends and she knows we can deal with it, especially with all of your help and with God's comfort He gives with His Holy Spirit. And He's given it in a great way.

To you who are planning to follow Roni's footsteps, or are there already, serving the Lord in full-time work, most of all those of you serving in a faraway place like Roni did, what would she say to you? . . . I think she'd say something along the lines of, "Stay close to God." And to those of you who are thinking of going to the mission field someday, she would say, "Obey. If you feel God is asking you to do something like that, don't run from Him; just obey. Or at least seek to know for sure and do it."

And then, of course, there's a group of people, maybe not many here tonight but all around the world, people who don't know Jesus Christ as their Savior, who have no confidence that they would go to heaven one day. They're trying hard, some of them, to please God, but they haven't admitted their guilt of rebellion against God. What would Roni say to you? Maybe something that I've said many times to our Peruvian friends . . . I think she would say something like, "Please, all of you, please, please don't leave matters of eternity up to chance." The most important issue of our life we leave to chance. Isn't that ridiculous?

So I ask you tonight, in Roni's behalf, those of you who don't know the Savior who Roni knows and is enjoying tonight, please seek God, and God will show Himself to you.

APPENDIX B

Text of Elisabeth Elliot Gren's recorded message, played at Roni and Charity Bowers's memorial service in Fruitport, Michigan, on April 27, 2001.

I have heard the story of Jim Bowers's loss of his wife and child who were shot down. It's one of those stunning things in life. You wonder what God is doing, and of course, we know that God never makes mistakes. He knows exactly what He is doing, and suffering is never for nothing. It says in 1 Thessalonians 3:4, "We are bound to suffer hardship," and Samuel Rutherford points out to us, "It is ordinary. It is a part of the cross. Suffering makes pleasure more poignant. It can only reveal the depth of Christ's love."

He has given to you, Jim, the cup of suffering; and you can share that with the Lord Jesus who said, "The cup the Father has given to me, I have received." In Philippians 1:29, Paul says, "It is given to you not only to believe but also to suffer."

I'm tempted to ask, "So what else is new?" All of us, in one form or another, are required to suffer. Some of us accept it graciously, trustingly; others rage against God about it. But God has reasons for needing those two precious people in His heavenly home. He has not forgotten you, Jim, or any of the others who are gathered around with you. Surely He has work for you to do that would not fit anyone else. It says in Psalm 90:12, "Teach us to number our days aright, that we may gain a heart of wisdom." It is my prayer that the Lord would do just that for you and for all those who share your sorrow.

George MacDonald, the Scottish writer, wrote, "Were it not for suffering, millions of human beings would never develop an atom of affection. It is folly to conclude that a thing ought not to be done because it hurts. There are powers to be born, creations to be perfected, sinners to be redeemed all through the ministry of pain that could be born, perfected, and redeemed in no other way."

I'd like to conclude with a beautiful poem written by Martha Snell Nicholson:

"I stood a mendicant (a beggar) of God before His royal throne
And begged Him for one priceless gift, which I could call my own.
I took the gift from out His hand, but as I would depart
I cried, 'But, Lord, this is a thorn and it has pierced my heart.
This is a strange, a hurtful gift, which Thou hast given me.'
He said, 'My child, I give good gifts and gave My best to thee.'
I took it home and though at first the cruel thorn hurt sore,
As long years passed I learned at last to love it more and more.
I learned He never gives a thorn without this added grace,
He takes the thorn to pin aside the veil which hides His face."

APPENDIX C

Text of speech given by Steve Saint at Roni and Charity Bowers's memorial service in Fruitport, Michigan, on April 27, 2001.

Cory, my name is Steve. You know what? A long time ago when I was just about your size, I was in a meeting just like this. I was sitting down there, and I really didn't know completely what was going on. But I was surrounded by people that I called aunt and uncle. They weren't all my family, but they really were like my family. And my mom was there and Aunt Mary Lou and Aunt Barb and Aunt Betty (the lady that just talked by recording).

And you know, I was trying to figure out what was going on. We had just had Christmas, and here all these people were coming back to our house, and I thought, *Maybe we're going to have Christmas again*. There were a lot of people crying and some people seemed to be sad. But in the midst of all that, there were other people laughing and I knew that something good was about to happen; I just didn't know what it was.

You know, people have asked me about that, Cory, and I tell them that I didn't really understand what was going on. But you know, now I understand it better. A lot of adults used a word then that I didn't understand. They used a word that's called tragedy. And when tragic things happen, adults do really interesting things. They cry and sometimes they can be happy and sad at the same time.

And these people were saying that what had happened before we came to that church service was something tragic. But you know, now I'm kind of an old guy, and now when people come to me and they say, "Oh, I remember when that tragedy happened so long ago," I know, Cory, that they were wrong. You see, my dad, who was a pilot like the man you probably call Uncle Kevin, and four of his really good friends had just been buried out in the jungle, and my mom told me that my dad was never coming home again. My mom wasn't really sad. So I asked her, "Where did my dad go?"

And she said, "He went to live with Jesus."

And you know, that's where my mom and dad had told me that we all wanted to go and live. Well, I thought, *Isn't that great that Daddy got to go sooner than the rest of us?* And you know what? Now when people say, "That was a tragedy," I know they are wrong.

In life, many of us Christians have tried to preach and have tried to believe that the life of a believer is all joy and no pain. That isn't so. And we've tried to believe that for those people who don't know the Lord as we do, their life is all pain and no joy, and that isn't so. You know what the difference is (and it's taken me a long time to learn it)? For them, the pain is fundamental and the joy is superficial because it won't last. For us, the pain is superficial and the joy is fundamental.

A good friend of mine, Steve Curtis Chapman, wrote a song taken from 1 Thessalonians 4:13–14 and I give this to you. He wrote,

"This is not how we thought it was supposed to be.
We had so many plans for you. We had so many dreams.
And now you've gone away leaving us with nothing
    but the memories of your smile.

And nothing we can say and nothing we can do
can take away the pain, the pain of losing you.
But we cry with hope, and we say good-bye with hope
because we know our good-bye is not the end.
We can grieve with hope because we believe with hope,
there's a place where we'll see your face again."

Cory, I had a little girl who had grown up to be a big, tall, beautiful girl. She was the only little girl that I had, and I loved her so much. Just a few months ago she had been away on missions just like your daddy and mommy and you and your little sister were. And when she came home, we met her at the airport. We had these signs saying "Welcome home, Stephanie," (that was her name). We lifted them up in the air.

One of my friends from the jungle was there with us and he had his sign upside down because he couldn't read. Everybody was looking at us, even though we were in Orlando and people do funny things there.

And you know what? We went home and we were having a party, a welcome home party. And Cory, Stephanie got a headache and went to lie down. My wife, Jenny, asked me to go in and pray for her. And you know what happened? While Jenny was holding Stephanie and I was praying for her, she died.

And you know what, Cory? We had just had a little grandbaby. Stephanie's older brother, my son Jessie, had just had a baby. And when Stephanie came home, she wanted to hold that baby. She was so excited; she wouldn't let anybody else hold the baby because she wanted her chance with our little baby. She loved babies so much.

And when I think of our Stephanie, one of the things that makes me saddest is that she didn't get to hold her little niece very much. And you know what I thought when I heard on the radio that your mommy and baby sister had gone to live with Jesus a little sooner than we thought they would? I thought, "Oh, thank You, Jesus." Because I'll bet if there's anything that's like a problem in heaven, you know what it is? It's that my daughter Stephanie is just going to be bugging your mother all of the time to hold your little sister, Charity.

Cory, we sing a song, and I know you know it: "Jesus Loves Me, This I Know." You know that one, don't you? You know what? I'd like to change the second line to, "Jesus Loves Me, this I know, because fifty years now (that's how old I am) have proved it so." And Cory, I believe that when you're as old as I am that you'll understand like I do now, Jesus never wastes a hurt. We can't prove our faith nearly so well as we can right now.

Appendix D

Text of Steve Green's comments and song from Roni and Charity Bowers's memorial service in Fruitport, Michigan, on April 27, 2001.

Along with friends, family, and loved ones who are gathered, I wish to extend my deepest, heartfelt condolences. In times like these, perhaps we sense most keenly that mysterious union of belonging to Christ, of being knit together as His body. All over the world, thousands of believers are lifting you up in prayer and sharing in your grief in a way that far surpasses human sympathy. Also in times like these, the hope of the gospel shines brightly and provides hope when hope cannot be found in any other place.

Thank you for serving our Lord so faithfully. You lived in obscurity. You served Him in obscurity, but you are highly favored in His sight, for: "Beautiful are the feet of those who take the gospel of good news" [see Romans 10:15].

Thank you for your part in the kingdom. May the Lord continue to surround you with His comfort and His grace.

I WILL SERVE THE LORD

There marches through the centuries
The martyrs of the cross,
All those who chose to follow Christ,
To suffer any loss.
And though their journey led them
Through the shadowlands of death,
The song of their commitment
They rehearsed with every breath.

Chorus:
I will serve the Lord.
I will serve the Lord, my God.
And if God should choose
And my life I lose,
Though my foe may slay me,
I will serve the Lord.

Uncertain days now echo back
That strong and urgent strain,
To count the cost, take up the cross
And join in the refrain.
For should our journey lead us through
The shadowlands of death,
May this be our hearts' resolve
As long as we have breath:

Chorus:
I will serve the Lord.
I will serve the Lord, my God.
And if God should choose
And my life I lose,
Though my foe may slay me,
I will serve the Lord.

The honor and the privilege ours;
With wounds we suffer by His side.
And to the glory of the Lord,
Those sacred scars we wear with pride.

Chorus:
I will serve the Lord.
I will serve the Lord, my God.
And if God should choose
And my life I lose,
Though my foe may slay me,
I will serve the Lord.

NOTES

Chapter Three

1. Description of program taken from "Memorandum of Justification for Presidential Determination Regarding the Resumption of U.S. Aerial Tracking Information Sharing and Other Assistance to the Government of Peru" and Presidential Determination 95-9, December 8, 1994. Annex C and D of "Review of U.S. Assistance to Peruvian Counter-Drug Air Interdiction Efforts and the Shootdown of a Civilian Aircraft on April 20, 2001." Report of Select Committee on Intelligence, U.S. Senate, October 2001.
2. Ibid.
3. "Review of U.S. Assistance to Peruvian Counter-Drug Air Interdiction Efforts and the Shootdown of a Civilian Aircraft on April 20, 2001." Report of Select Committee on Intelligence, U.S. Senate, October 2001.

Chapter Four

1. "Transcript of Videotape of OB-1408 Incident, Peru Investigation Report: The April 20, 2001 Peruvian Shootdown Accident," August 20, 2001.
2. Ibid.

Chapter Five

1. "Transcript of Videotape of OB-1408 Incident, Peru Investigation Report: The April 20, 2001 Peruvian Shootdown Accident," August 20, 2001.

Chapter Six

1. "Transcript of Videotape of OB-1408 Incident, Peru Investigation Report: The April 20, 2001 Peruvian Shootdown Accident," August 20, 2001.
2. Ibid.

Chapter Fourteen

1. "Good Morning America," April 23, 2001. America's Broadcasting Company.
2. "A Bolt Out of the Blue," Prime Time Thursday, May 24, 2001. America's Broadcasting Company.

Moody Press, a ministry of Moody Bible Institute,
is designed for education, evangelization, and edification.
If we may assist you in knowing more about Christ
and the Christian life, please write us without obligation:
Moody Press, c/o MLM, Chicago, Illinois 60610.

FRANCISCO DE ORELLANA
PUCALLPA
INDIANA
APAYACU
HUANTA
PEBAS
Amazon River
IQUITOS
Amazon River
L
O
R
M A R I S C A L
RÍO NAPO